WRITER-FILES

General Editor: Simon Trussler

Associate Editor: Malcolm Page

File on
AYCKBOURN

Compiled by Malcolm Page

Methuen Drama

A Methuen Drama Book

First published in 1989 as a paperback original
by Methuen Drama, Michelin House,
81 Fulham Road, London SW3 6RB
and HEB Inc., 70 Court Street, Portsmouth
New Hampshire 03801, USA

Copyright in the compilation
©1989 by Malcolm Page
Copyright in the series format
©1989 by Methuen Drama
Copyright in the editorial presentation
©1989 by Simon Trussler

Typeset in 9/10 Times
by L. Anderson Typesetting
Woodchurch, Kent TN26 3TB

Printed in Great Britain by
Richard Clay Ltd, Bungay, Suffolk

British Library Cataloguing in Publication Data

Page, Malcolm, 1935-
    File on Ayckbourn — (Writer-files)
    1. Drama in English. Ayckbourn, Alan, 1938- . Critical studies
    I. Title   II. Series
    822'.914

    ISBN 0-413-42010-8

Contents

Acknowledgement

My grateful thanks to Heather Stoney, of the
Stephen Joseph Theatre-in-the-Round, who
answered my many questions helpfully and
promptly.

Malcolm Page

The theatre is, by its nature, an ephemeral art: yet it is a daunting task to track down the newspaper reviews, or contemporary statements from the writer or his director, which are often all that remain to help us recreate some sense of what a particular production was like. This series is therefore intended to make readily available a selection of the comments that the critics made about the plays of leading modern dramatists at the time of their production — and to trace, too, the course of each writer's own views about his work and his world.

In addition to combining a uniquely convenient source of such elusive *documentation*, the 'Writer-Files' series also assembles the *information* necessary for readers to pursue further their interest in a particular writer or work. Variations in quantity between one writer's output and another, differences in temperament which make some readier than others to talk about their work, and the variety of critical response, all mean that the presentation and balance of material shifts between one volume and another: but we have tried to arrive at a format for the series which will nevertheless enable users of one volume readily to find their way around any other.

Section 1, 'A Brief Chronology', provides a quick conspective overview of each playwright's life and career. *Section 2* deals with the plays themselves, arranged chronologically in the order of their composition: information on first performances, major revivals, and publication is followed by a brief synopsis (for quick reference set in slightly larger, italic type), then by a representative selection of the critical response, and of the dramatist's own comments on the play and its theme.

Section 3 offers concise guidance to each writer's work in non-dramatic forms, while *Section 4*, 'The Writer on His Work', brings together comments from the playwright himself on more general matters of construction, opinion, and artistic development. Finally, *Section 5* provides a bibliographical guide to other primary and secondary sources of further reading, among which full details will be found of works cited elsewhere under short titles, and of collected editions of the plays — but not of individual titles, particulars of which will be found with the other factual data in Section 2.

The 'Writer-Files' hope by striking this kind of balance between information and a wide range of opinion to offer 'companions' to the study of major playwrights in the modern repertoire — not in that dangerous pre-digested fashion which can too readily quench the desire to read the plays themselves, nor so prescriptively as to allow any single line of approach to predominate, but rather to encourage readers to form their own judgements of the plays in a wide-ranging context.

Alan Ayckbourn, on separate occasions recorded in this volume, has described both comedy and farce as 'tragedies that have been interrupted': and it is a measure of how accustomed we have of late become to 'dark' or 'black' comedy that this inversion of the traditional expectations of the comic genres should have been so little remarked. Like a non-political Priestley, Ayckbourn writes apparently conventional plays about apparently conventional people which yet express a profound unease about the very structure of the universe — and times and places become inextricably meshed as naturalistic determinism dissolves before the infinite potentiality of Ayckbourn's theatrical version of quantum theory. Yet at one level (the word is chosen advisedly) what is he doing but substituting for the multiple doors of traditional farce — denied him by the in-the-round staging for which his work is first conceived — his own kind of dimensional multiplicity, in which it becomes impossible to disentangle stage mechanics from metaphysics as he presents us with starkly symmetrical views of his asymmetrical universe?

Ayckbourn has a habit of choosing conversational clichés for the titles of his plays — and his characters, too, are dependent upon the small-change of dramatic dialogue, their real feelings deeply hidden in the subtext. Almost all are quite incapable of traversing the boundaries of their circumscribed lives: and I was struck by Robert Cushman's remark on page 52 that Ayckbourn 'sees his people less in terms of character than terms of domestic circumstance' — so that niceties of individual psychology are sacrificed to one's sense of appalling typicality. It is this shocked recognition which refuses to Ayckbourn's audiences the usual, satisfying 'closure' effected by comedy — this, and the discomfiting awareness that they are still surrounded by his characters as they jostle their way out of the theatre, board their trains home, and even, perish the thought, as they enter their own kitchen-dinettes.

As Ayckbourn's career has progressed, the veneer of jokiness has been steadily chipped away until, as Bernard Levin puts it on page 45, his characters begin to resemble 'real people in real pain'. I am not sure that it is necessarily more 'grown up', as Levin suggests, thus to dramatize suburban angst rather than to laugh joyfully, whether in the face of existential terror or of faux-pas at a dinner-party: but it is certainly a kind of self-recognition on the dramatist's part, an edging ever closer to the 'tragic ending' that keeps being interrupted by the comedy.

Simon Trussler

1939 12 April, born in Hampstead; father a violinist, mother a writer of romantic novels.

1946 Weekly boarder at local boarding school. Mother re-marries a bank manager: lives in Billingshurst, Wisborough Green, Horsham, Uckfield, Hayward's Heath, and Lewes.

1951 To Haileybury School on Barclay's Bank Scholarship. 'It was a very tough school. ... There's a way to do it and that's to play the system and create your own niche. And it sounds madly pretentious, but we formed a sort of bohemian section. ... I wasn't too bad at cricket and I was an average rugby player. ... I used to write the house play at the end of every term. ... I also edited the house magazine' (*Conversations*, 26-7). Toured the Netherlands in the school production of *Romeo and Juliet* in 1955 ('That was magic. That was the first real "theatre" theatre I'd experienced', *Conversations*, 24) and toured in eastern U.S. and Canada as Macduff in *Macbeth* in 1956.

1956 Left school with 'A' levels in English and History. Acting ASM with Sir Donald Wolfit's production of *The Strong are Lonely* at Edinburgh Festival. Unpaid student ASM, with bit parts, at Worthing.

1957 Weekly rep. at Leatherhead, acting and stage-managing. Summer season with theatre-in-the-round, directed by Stephen Joseph, Scarborough. Winter season at Oxford Playhouse as stage manager and actor ('You can get any amount of bloody actors, but stage managers are terribly rare, and people who were actually able to understand all this machinery were like gold dust. I was beginning to get quite good at it', *Conversations*, 33).

1958-59 Summer seasons at Scarborough, and winter tours by the company to Leicester, Wellingborough, Hemel Hempstead, and Stoke.

1959 His first two performed plays, *The Square Cat* and *Love after All*, both as 'Roland Allen', at Scarborough. Married Christine Roland, actress: they had two sons, and separated some years later.

1960 Succeeds in obtaining medical discharge from RAF after two days at Cardington. *Dad's Tale* ('Roland Allen') at Scarborough.

1961 *Standing Room Only* ('Roland Allen') at Scarborough.

1962   Founder-member and Associate Director of Victoria Theatre (in-the-round), Stoke-on-Trent, directed by Peter Cheeseman. *Xmas vs. Mastermind* at Stoke. Parts he played here included Vladimir in *Waiting for Godot*, More in *A Man for All Seasons* and Bill Starbuck in *The Rainmaker*.

1963   *Mr. Whatnot* at Stoke (London, 1964).

1964   Last appearance as an actor in *Two for the Seesaw* (William Gibson), Rotherham. Joined BBC, Leeds, as radio drama producer, staying till 1970. 'I found [radio] was a magic place. At that particular point in the history of the BBC, it was such a backwater (television was the place) that you could work totally unobserved doing the most interesting things. It did two things: it gave me a great opportunity to do far more plays — I did more plays in a year than I'd done in ten years in the theatre — and it also foisted upon me the occasional plays that I didn't want to do, which, of course, in the theatre you can generally avoid' (*Conversations*, 103).

1965-69   Combined summer seasons writing and directing at Scarborough with BBC work. 1965: *Meet my Father* (London, 1967, re-titled *Relatively Speaking*). 1967: *The Sparrow*. 1969: *How the Other Half Loves* (London, 1970). 'Countdown,' sketch, performed as part of *Mixed Doubles*, London. *Ernie's Incredible Illucinations* published.

1970   Became Director of Productions at Library Th., Scarborough. *The Story So Far* at Scarborough.

1971   *Time and Time Again* (London, 1972).

1972   *Absurd Person Singular* (London, 1973).

1973   *The Norman Conquests* (London, 1974).

1974   *Absent Friends* (London, 1975). *Confusions* (London, 1976). *Service Not Included*, written for television, presented.

1975   *Bedroom Farce* (London, 1977). *Jeeves*, musical (London, 1976).

1976   *Just between Ourselves* (London, 1977). Company moved into Stephen Joseph Th., Scarborough, and began year-round operation.

1977   *Ten Times Table* (London, 1978).

1978   *Joking Apart* (London, 1979). *Men on Women on Men*, first revue, with music by Paul Todd.

1979   *Sisterly Feelings* (London, 1980). *Taking Steps* (London, 1980).

1980   *Suburban Strains*, with music by Paul Todd (London, with

Scarborough company, 1981). *First Course* and *Second Helping*, revues. *Season's Greetings* (London, with Scarborough Company, 1980; 1982).

1981   *Way Upstream* (London, 1982). *Making Tracks* (London, 1983). *Me, Myself and I*, three linked lunch-time shows (London, 1982).

1982   *Intimate Exchanges* (London, 1984). *A Trip to Scarborough.*

1983   *It Could Be Any One of Us. Incidental Music*, revue (also London).

1984   *A Chorus of Disapproval* (London, 1985). *Seven Deadly Virtues*, revue. *The Westwoods*, three linked lunch-time shows (London, 1987).

1985   *A Woman in Mind* (London, 1986). *Boy Meets Girl* and *Girl Meets Boy*, two linked lunch-time revues.

1986   *Mere Soup Songs*, revue. Left Scarborough for two years to work at National Th., London, initially directing *Tons of Money* and *'Tis Pity She's a Whore.*

1987   His National Theatre production of *A View from the Bridge* at the Cottesloe achieves wide critical acclaim, transfers to the Aldwych, and receives numerous awards, including the *Plays and Players* Award for Best Director. Also receives *Evening Standard* Best Play Award for the National Theatre production of *A Small Family Business*, which he also directed. At Scarborough, directs *Henceforward* ... (London, 1988).

1988   *Man of the Moment. A Chorus of Disapproval* filmed in Scarborough.

a: Stage Plays

The Square Cat

A play by 'Roland Allen'.
First production: Library Th., Scarborough, 30 July 1959.
Unpublished and not available for production.

It was about a family — it sounds terribly banal — about a husband, his wife, his son and his daughter. The mother has got an obsession with a pop singer. She's fallen in love with him from a distance, thinks he's wonderful and swoony. She therefore rents a house in the country (a little Anouilh coming out there: there were a lot of definite influences in this play. In fact it's Dinner with the Family, *I now realize!) in order to invite the pop singer down for a marvellous weekend with her. And she was going to pretend to be someone totally different; have no family, and be a rich woman — she'd arranged it all. ... I don't quite know why he comes, but anyway he agrees to come, we find out later. The family has followed her down and is not going to let mother get away as easily as that. They say: 'All right, let him come.' She's very cross and says: 'No, you've spoiled the whole thing.' He turns up — that's me — and of course he's not at all the glittering figure of the silver screen, but shy and bespectacled and wanting a quiet time — and this he thought was it. And he's horrified to see that mother is a sort of elderly groupie. The family roars with merriment saying: 'Look, you see, look at your hero. He's really nothing very much.' At which point he bounds out and comes back again in a glitter costume, twanging his guitar, saying: 'OK, this is war' — or words to that effect (I can't remember much of the plot). He gets together with the daughter eventually, and romance blossoms there. Mother finds the error of her ways and goes back to her husband. Jerry Ross finds true love with the simple girl, and all fades into the sunset.*

I don't think it was very good as a play, looking back on it, but it was OK for a first one. ... It was farce. I think it comes under the term farce, because there was a lot of leaping about and mistaken identities in it. It was certainly as broad as I got for quite some time. It was curious, because I didn't sit down to write anything particularly, except a play. I'd been writing before that, but they'd never had the test of production, and most of them, with a couple of exceptions which had been rather morose pieces, had been comic in tone. ... It made me forty-seven quid, I remember, more than I earned in several weeks.

Ayckbourn, *Conversations*, p. 51-2

Love after All

A play by 'Roland Allen'.
First production: Library Th., Scarborough, 21 Dec. 1959.
Unpublished and not available for production.

A gay, new farce, in Edwardian days, of love, folly and disguise. The father, a mean old cuss, wants to marry his daughter off to a rich heir. Oddly enough, he succeeds! But true love does win, just the same.

It was obviously going to be a period thing, because it was based on *The Barber of Seville*. I remember seeing the play at school. The suitor keeps coming back and disguising himself, getting in as a music teacher. I tinkered around with it a lot. And in the first version, with Clifford Williams directing, it was a very good production — it was very tight and quite fun, and we did it Edwardian.

Ayckbourn, *Conversations*, p. 57

Dad's Tale

A comedy by 'Roland Allen'.
First production: Library Th., Scarborough, 19 Dec. 1960
    (dir. Clifford Williams).
Unpublished and not available for production.

The story is told by Martin, an interior decorator, and looks back to his own family's Christmas five years ago: a rags-to riches Christmas that begins in abject poverty and that ends with a feast of plenty because Martin's Dad claims a £250 reward on some stolen silverware which a friend has dumped on him just as he is about to be nicked.

Michael Billington, *Alan Ayckbourn*, p. 7

It was written for two companies, us and the British Dance Drama Theatre, who weren't going to meet until very late on in rehearsals. Clifford was directing our company; Gerard Bagley was directing the dance company. And what I had to do was write the play overall, then write separately the story that the ballet should take. ... It was quite an adventurous show. ... It was not a success (a) because I think we were into a winter season in Scarborough, which never established itself; and (b) because it was a children's play.

Ayckbourn, *Conversations*, p. 57-8

Standing Room Only

A comedy in three acts (revised version in two acts) by
    'Roland Allen'.
First production: Library Th., Scarborough, 13 July 1961.
Unpublished and not available for production.

He postulates a London of the future in which a tremendous traffic jam brings everything to a halt. ... Londoners are immobilized where the jam leaves them; people camp out in cars and buses throughout the West End. The plot focuses on one family living for years in a double-decker bus.

Sidney Howard White, *Alan Ayckbourn*, p. 16

It is a simple, cheerful, friendly play that takes an Absurdist situation of a society that has ground to a halt (later used not only by Peter Nichols [in *The Freeway*] but also by Jean-Luc Godard in his film *Weekend*) and shows how even so the urge to carry on the race continues.

Michael Billington, *Alan Ayckbourn*, p. 11

Xmas vs. Mastermind

A children's' play.
First production: Victoria Th., Stoke-on-Trent, Dec. 1961
   (dir Peter Cheeseman; with Ayckbourn in cast).
Unpublished and not available for production.

---

*It was a play about Father Christmas, who was actually a very
unpleasant old man. He was faced with industrial trouble. His
chief gnome had called the men out. The gnome was inspired by
an evil character called the Crimson Golliwog, who was not
that at all, but who had a special gang whose object was to take
over Father Christmas anyway. They incited the gnome to this
revolutionary action just before Christmas and also abducted
his fairy helper. It was quite a broad, jolly farce, with lots of
fights in telephone boxes. And there were two policemen, who
tracked everything down, disguised as hedges and letter boxes.*

Ayckbourn, *Conversations*, p. 58

Mr. Whatnot

A play in two acts.
First production: Victoria Th., Stoke-on-Trent, November 1963
   (dir. Ayckbourn).
First London production: Arts Th., 6 Aug. 1964 (dir. Warren Jenkins;
   with Peter King as Mr. Whatnot, Ronnie Barker as Lord Slingsby-
   Craddock, Judy Campbell as his wife, Marie Lohr as Mrs. Grisley-
   Williams, and Judy Cornwell as Agnes).
Published: London: Samuel French.

---

*Mr. Whatnot, a piano tuner, with a touch of the Little Man but,
more important, independence, determination, strength and a
great sense of humour is called to see to the Slingsby-
Craddock's grand piano. The play consists of his reactions to
the Slingsby-Craddocks and their friends and their reactions to
him, out of this arising a series of highly amusing and frequently
very witty comments, usually made in the sign language of*

13

movement and sound that Mr. Ayckbourn manages so finely. The old grunting peer, his younger, bored wife, the daughter and her silly-ass boy-friend, the family butler, a bizarre maid, and a tweedy neighbour, are somehow inspired by Mr. Whatnot to enact aspects of their lives which are serious to them but fundamentally trivial in the extreme. There is a wonderful game of tennis and another of billiards, entirely in mime. Tea and conversation are carried on as if hanging in the air. Mr. Whatnot has a splendid time confusing the family at dinner table, when he switches the glasses of wine. He also has his eye on the daughter, and she on him. ...

Ayckbourn demolishes the whose-for-tennis upper class in a way that reminds one of John Osborne in *The World of Paul Slickey* but with sufficient of his own imagination and inventiveness to make one instantly take to his play.

R.B. M[arriott], 'Who's for Tennis?,' *The Stage*, 13 Aug. 1964, p. 7

We had an actor, Peter King, in his first season [at Stoke], who had a natural ability for mime: he was a very clean, clear, in fact a very strong mime actor, and I always thought that it would be nice to use him more in that context. Secondly, I've got a great fondness for silent film, all the old classics — particularly the Buster Keatons and Harold Lloyds and people like that, rather more than Chaplin. I'd also seen a couple of films by René Clair, particularly *Le Million*, which I was terribly taken with. ... *Whatnot* started by using common jargon from other media and transposing it into a theatre setting, something I've done quite a lot — things like the car chase and running across ploughed fields in the morning, and a lot of filmic sequences of lovers in the sunset, and operas, and people dining in restaurants with gipsy violinists. ... I originally wanted to write it with no dialogue at all. And, in fact, when I wrote the dialogue I asked the actors to learn it and then distort it; so that 'Jolly nice day!' would become: 'Wah-wah wah wah!' and so on. However, when they were playing the dialogue, it actually was quite funny, and they were rather reluctant to let some of it go. ... Silence in a character creates a richness of its own. ... I've seen a great variety in the Whatnots over the years. Paul Moriarty played him: it was a wonderful performance, he was a very good Whatnot. But it was a totally different, more dangerous, manic Whatnot that he played. Peter King is Welsh — he was a Welsh Whatnot; they're very rapacious and his was a very sexy Whatnot. ...

Almost everything went wrong with the London production. ... The balance of the cast and the director itself was wrong. The second thing that was wrong was that it was over-produced, and that far too much money was spent on it. ...

I think of the *Whatnot* theme as being the Id figure who bounds along, the one inside me that would like to up-end and destroy — not destroy gratuitously, just to up-end, really, and confuse a little, upset *status quos*.

Ayckbourn, *Conversations*, p. 64-8, 40

It has, too, social principles: it believes that plebeian vigour, sincerity and enterprise will conquer a decadent aristocracy left behind from some earlier period of innocence when the upper classes talked and dressed like the creations of Mr. P.G. Wodehouse in their less inspired moments.

Anon., 'Theatre of Ridiculous', *The Times*, 7 Oct. 1964, p. 14

Take the most effete, upper crust, Blandings Castle-ish set up you can think of; present it in theatrical cartoon strip with all its eccentricities to the fore; inject into this nutty world a humble Walter Mitty-ing piano tuner (as it might be a creature from a different planet, allowed to communicate only in mime — a figure from *commedia dell'arte*) like a spanner in the works. Contrive that many scenes be swiftly cross cut in the manner of silent cinema (indeed see that it ends with a Keystone Cops chase in unreliable motor cars); also, that sound and vision often complement rather than match one another (never mind the horrific timing problems, in production). You might, if you are as clever as Alan Ayckbourn, end up with something like *Mr. Whatnot*: a good-natured dig at the ineffably self-centred world of the stately home set. Alan Ayckbourn without words — almost.

Cordelia Oliver, *The Guardian*, Oct. 1976
[production at Ochtertyre]

Relatively Speaking

A play in two acts, originally titled *Meet My Father*.
First production: Library Th., Scarborough, 8 July 1965.
First London production: Duke of York's Th., 29 Mar. 1967
  (dir. Nigel Patrick; with Michael Hordern as Philip, Celia Johnson as Sheila, and Richard Briers as Greg).
First American production: Arena Stage, Washington, June 1974.
Revival: Greenwich Th., 7 Apr. 1986 (dir. Alan Strachan; with
  Michael Aldridge as Philip, and Gwen Watford as Sheila).
Television: BBC-1, 2 Mar. 1969 (dir. Herbert Wise).
Published: London: Evans Plays, 1968.

Ayckbourn juggles with four characters: an unmarried young pair linked to a middle-aged couple by the girl's affair with the husband. Now she wants to drop him and retrieve her letters: accordingly she visits him in the country where she finds the boy already making himself at home on the assumption that the couple are her parents. It is a threadbare pretext for bringing them all together, and no one realizes this more clearly than the author who invariably calculates to a hair's breadth just how much obtuseness his audience will tolerate on behalf of the situations it precipitates.

The play is a house of cards, always just escaping collapse. Most of the action takes place in duologues working through every permutation of misunderstanding with the exhaustiveness of a computer: rarely has dramatic irony been so thoroughly exploited in a single play. ... Ayckbourn performs over the old marital territory, but he has no point to make about adultery or erotic betrayal — least of all the implicit moral judgments which used to underprop commercial comedy. He tackles the theme simply as a game to be played as brilliantly as possible.

Irving Wardle, 'Fun down to the Last Drop',
The Times, 30 Mar. 1967, p. 10

The people who liked this play when it was first seen remarked that it was 'well constructed'; those that didn't called it old-fashioned. If the latter is true, then I suppose it's because, as the song goes, I am too. As to whether it's well constructed, well, in a way I hope it is, since I did set out consciously to write a 'well-made' play. I think this is important for a playwright to do at least once in his life, since as in any science, he cannot begin to shatter theatrical convention or break golden rules until he is reasonably sure in himself what they are and how they were arrived at. ... Stephen Joseph ... asked me then simply for a play which would make people laugh when their seaside summer holidays were spoiled by the rain and they came into the theatre to get dry before trudging back to their landladies. This seemed to me as worthwhile a reason for writing a play as any, so I tried to comply. I hope I have succeeded.

Ayckbourn, 'Introduction,' *Relatively Speaking*,
(Evans Plays, 1968), p. iii

Ayckbourn has no message, nothing to peddle except an infectious delight in the absurdities of English manners. This wouldn't be so worrying if the play were not also, by our standards, unnaturally deft — as slick as the best of Broadway. ... Ayckbourn is not particularly interested in character, or only in so far as each of his four types represents an aspect of the English character, out of which their situation arises — an ingenious, airy structure of misunderstanding, diffidence, hair breadth escapes from tactlessness, and the subtle, desperate ruses to which the polite are driven in order to avoid appearing gauche. His amusement at these foibles has a certain timelessness, and his plot might have been lifted from the eighteenth century.

Hilary Spurling, 'Farewell the Hairy Men',
Spectator, 7 Apr. 1967, p. 402-3

An aridly ingenious mistaken-identity farce that begins in utter fatuity, but ascends in time to the merely inane. ... Perhaps it failed to amuse me because it is fatuous.

Julius Novick, 'Two Plays at Washington's Arena Stage',
New York Times, 14 July 1974, Sec. II, p. 3

He just happens to be a dazzling comic writer who uses language with the precision, freshness and economy of Wodehouse or Pinter. Arnold Bennett's early reference to Coward as 'our modern Congreve' could more fairly be applied to Ayckbourn for his lovingly detailed sense of character and fastidious use of haunting verbal clichés to help build the very structure of a situation. *Relatively Speaking* is a faultless mechanism for four players, replete with the usual distorting mirror transversals and delicately tense crescendos of uncomprehending, lunatically cross-purposed exchanges of which Beckett, with his famous love for vaudeville routines, could well be envious. One of many signs of Ayckbourn's special grace as a writer is the way in which the true nastiness of his domestic tyrants or hypocrites is screened from us, until we are going home, by the sheer humour and barminess of those verbal exchanges on stage, which seem as brightly lit as the set itself. Our delighted sympathy is engaged by such sharp and cunning use of simple language with all its hesitancies, pauses and flurries of sound. Only later does the contour of a domestic monster become apparent.

Bryan Robertson, 'Bright Revivals', *Spectator*, 4 Sept. 1982, p. 25
[on Theatre on the Green touring production, Richmond]

He gives us a classic comedy in two acts and four scenes.
Scene I: We meet couple A. *Scene II:* We meet couple B. *Scene III:* Sparks fly when the two couples meet. *Scene IV:* All is resolved and the participants are sadder but wiser as a result. Using this classic pattern, not dissimilar to *Private Lives* for instance, the laughter is sporadic in

the first scene, frequent in the second, continuous in the third, with concentrated chuckles in the fourth. ... And the moral you should take home with you? That marriage, as Stevenson said, is a field of battle and not a bed of roses. ... But you knew that already. That the first lie is usually disastrous, because it is likely to lead to an enormity of lying? But you knew that too. That beneath the gentility of the home counties, white hot passions are subversively at work? But everyone knows that. I think the moral is that Ayckbourn was, is, and will remain the most accurate and the funniest archivist of middle-class England during the farcical years since Macmillan came to power.

David Benedictus, *Plays International*, June 1986, p. 23-4

The Sparrow

A comedy in two acts.
First production: Library Th., Scarborough, 10 July 1967.
Unpublished.

We see Ed, a mild little bus conductor with a passion for boat-building, bringing the drenched, mini-skirted Evie back to his squalid flat after a night at the local ballroom. But, after a good deal of comic sparring, the tone changes with the arrival of Tony who owns the flat and who is everything Ed is not: smooth, brutal, authoritative. ... What follows in the next two scenes is a traditional sexual takeover. ... In the final scene, the real nature of the power struggle becomes clear. ... The one serious flaw in the play (rare in Ayckbourn) is that he wrenches human behaviour in accordance with the demands of his theme.

Michael Billington, *Alan Ayckbourn*, p. 27-8

I don't believe, in retrospect, that it's as good a play as *Relatively*, but it's only had three weeks in its life, those three weeks at Scarborough. It's probably worth a little more than that. At the time, the only reason it was suppressed was that somebody said it was a bit like *The Knack*. I didn't realize. I've seen *The Knack* since. It *is* a bit like *The Knack* — it's got a girl in the lead, that's what it was. But then, so has *Antony and Cleopatra*.

Ayckbourn, *Conversations*, p. 76

Countdown

Ten-minute duologue.
First production: in *We Who Are About To*, Hampstead Th. Club, 6 Feb.
  1969 (dir. Alexander Dore; with Nigel Stock as the Husband, and
  Vivien Merchant as the Wife); transferred to Comedy Th., 9 Apr.
  1969, retitled *Mixed Doubles*.
Published: in *Mixed Doubles* (Methuen, 1970).

---

*One of eight playlets making up 'an entertainment on marriage'.
Concerns two old people, the comic becoming pathetic. They
suppress the way each other's little habits and familiar phrases
irritate them: most of the lines are spoken thoughts.*

How the Other Half Loves

A play in two acts.
First production; Library Th., Scarborough, 31 July 1969
  (dir. Ayckbourn).
First London production: Lyric Th., 5 Aug. 1970 (dir. Robin Midgley;
  with Robert Morley as Frank).
First New York production: Royale Th., 29 Mar. 1971 (dir. Gene Saks;
  with Phil Silvers as Frank, and Sandy Dennis as Teresa).
Revival: Greenwich Th. (dir. Alan Strachan); transferred to Duke of
  York's Th., 8 June 1988.
Published: London: Evans Plays, 1971.

---

*The men in the play are linked by working for the same firm and
separated by nuances of position and background. At the top of
this particular social and business tree there is Frank Foster,
innately good-mannered even to plain ladies who ask for a tonic
water at cocktail time, who is saddled, at any rate in this
production, with an inexplicably tiresome American wife, Fiona,
played by Joan Tetzel with a brand of coy indestructibility that
one sometimes encounters in Harrods' food store. Fiona is
having a clandestine affair with Bob Phillips, who is rising up
the firm, comes — one suspects — from the suburban middle-*

19

classes, probably went to a Red Brick, and carries an impercep-
tible chip. He is married to Terry, who is very much a Guardian
graduate wife, always complaining about 'being stuck here all
day', hopeless with a child, a lousy cook, and who cuts bits out
of the paper and leaves them in piles instead of doing something
tidy — like going to the hairdressers. At the bottom of the tree
are the dupes: William Featherstone from the clerical end, who
says things like 'I took the liberty', and his mouse-wife, Mary. In
all, then, a pretty familiar bunch playing out the old chestnuts of
marital deception and red herrings. What gives the comedy its
only — and unique — distinction, is the brilliant central idea
(on a par, in its way, with Tom Stoppard's notion of building
Hamlet *round Rosencrantz and Guildenstern) of mixing the*
Fosters's drawing-room and the Phillips's living-room in the
same set, not by using the split screen technique of a semi-
dividing wall, but by entwining the two so that the sofa has
Foster cushions (Peter Jones) and Phillips cushions (Self-
ridges); the walls are patched in different colours, and in the
excruciating (and classic) dinner parties — the Featherstones
being guests at both — the table is laid with linen and paper
napkins, crystal and tumblers. This jumble-set is also an
extremely sharp device for having several people on stage
speaking apparently disconnected snatches of dialogue, talking
of each other almost in one another's faces through invisible
walls, and walking round each other in an early morning haze.
... There is, of course, Robert Morley, inevitably dominating the
stage from his first entrance in white running shorts. The lips
pout like a good-natured but put-upon baboon and, jowls over-
working, he delivers his lines as if he'd just thought of them and
found them delicious — 'We're out of bathroom stationery',
he gurgles.

Helen Dawson, *Plays and Players*, Oct. 1970, p. 38

I've always been interested in Time. Stage Time that is. How a writer is
able — and often does — bend time to suit his story telling 'Heavens',
cries some character, 'I've been here over an hour and nobody's even
offered me a drink.' In reality, of course, whilst it's an hour for the character, for the audience it's been only fifteen minutes. It's a device used
one way or another in practically every play that's ever been written. In
How the Other Half Loves, I've explored it a little more than is normal.

Similarly with Space. Stage Space that is. The same area of stage can be used to denote, say, a forest or a sitting room or a mineshaft — often with very little setting, particularly on the open stages that I normally use. Again, *How the Other Half Loves* plays around quite considerably with space. In fact, playing describes the whole piece rather exactly. The play's a game really which I hope an audience enjoys playing as much as the actors enjoy playing it.

> Ayckbourn, programme note,
> Channel Th. production, 1981

Fiona, in *How the Other Half*, is really a quite vicious character: she's not as vicious as some of her later versions, but she's an unfaithful wife who deceives her husband and plays a very sly game. ... A lot of *How the Other Half Loves* is about people getting extremely angry with each other. ...

I did meet a marvellous man called Gene Saks who was directing it [in New York], and with whom I hit it off immediately; and we sat down and with his advice I Americanized the script myself. It didn't help the play, in retrospect. At the time it was a very painless way to do it, because he just said: 'We would say that round the other way'. And as we did it, slowly we began to thin the language out and narrow down the subtleties.

> Ayckbourn, *Conversations*, p. 76-7, 79

The dazzling technique is not there as an end in itself but to service an idea; and one indicated by the punning title which obliquely refers both to one's marital partner and the class system. The play is very much about different styles of loving amongst the employers and the employed.

> Michael Billington, *Alan Ayckbourn*, p. 32

The essence of the play is surely incompatibility in marriage and inability, or otherwise, to cope. The upper-class Fosters live with it, she protected by an impermeable skin of self-esteem and he by opting out into easy-going, if occasionally troubled, absent-mindedness. The lower-middle Phillipses live in a perpetual domestic war zone, with squalid head-on collisions ending in brief sessions in bed.

> Cordelia Oliver, *The Guardian*, 14 July 1982
> [of the St. Andrews production]

Ernie's Incredible Illucinations

One-act play for children.

Television production: BBC-1, 11 Nov. 1987 (adapted Chris Borlas, dir. Colin Cant).

Published: French, 1969; in *Playbill One*, ed. Alan Durband (Hutchinson, 1969).

A bright comedy based on the extraordinary powers of Ernie Fraser, a day-dreamer with a difference. Like all schoolboys Ernie has a vivid imagination, but Ernie's thoughts have a disturbing habit of turning into reality. After a number of embarrassing episodes, Ernie's parents decide to consult a doctor, who is sceptical. Several of Ernie's adventures are acted out for us in flashback, but when Ernie fails to produce a Brass Band on demand, the doctor diagnoses group hallucination and recommends a visit to a specialist. However, 'Ernie's incredible illucinations' aren't to be dismissed quite so lightly.

Alan Durband, 'Introduction', *Playbill One*, p. 7

Family Circles

A comedy in two acts. Original title: *The Story So Far* (1970); revised as *Me Times Me Times Me* (1972); and as *Family Circles* (1978).

First production: Library Th., Scarborough, 20 Aug. 1970 (dir. Ayckbourn).

Revivals: 'pre-London' tour from 25 Aug. 1971 (dir. Robin Midgley); 'pre-London' tour from 13 Mar. 1972 (dir. Basil Coleman); Stephen Joseph Th., Scarborough, 4 Sept. 1985 (dir. Ayckbourn).

First London production: Orange Tree, Richmond, 17 Nov. 1978 (dir. Sam Walters).

Unpublished.

Three young couples come together for a parental wedding anniversary. Each is a type. Everyone seems unsuited. Glass turns up in sandwiches; there are mysterious 'accidents' and suspected nightcaps; and between the second and third acts they change partners while retaining their characters.

Eric Shorter, 'Regions', *Drama*, No. 99 (Winter 1970), p. 37-8

Me Times Me is probably not vintage, but it's got a few good laughs in it. ... In each act the daughter has a different husband and they change around; the premise of the play being that, depending on who you marry, you become slightly different. And it's quite fun to watch; but it got very complicated and no-one could understand it by the end of the play, because I brought all nine couples on — which made the people in Brighton extremely nervous. I'd hate to see it on Shaftesbury Avenue, because I think people would expect of it something it hasn't got.

Ayckbourn, interviewed by Ian Watson, 'Ayckbourn of Scarborough',
Municipal Entertainment, May 1978, p. 14

Emotionally, it is bleaker than any of his plays except *Just Between Ourselves*, and no less cynical about the domestic dovecote, the mock-Tudor love-nest. Once again, Ayckbourn is taking risks not easily reconciled with popular comedy. To a large extent, the canny observation and funny encounters justify those risks. As Ayckbourn sees it, the ugly sisters change awesomely little, whoever their partners may be. But one husband, resilient enough when he's married to the most bloody-minded, sinks into apathetic hypochondria when he moves on to the earnest, flustered one. Another, who flaunts a seedy grandeur when this fusspot is his wife, visibly coarsens when he's with the family flibbertygibbet and actually becomes violent when he's taken over by the commuter-belt Regan. This is revealing and instructive as far as it goes. The trouble is that we've hardly got a bearing on any relationship before it has flashed past.

Benedict Nightingale, *New Statesman*, 1 Dec. 1978, p. 763

Time and Time Again

A play in two acts.
First production: Library Th., Scarborough, 8 July 1971
 (dir. Ayckbourn).
First London production: Comedy Th., 16 Aug. 1972
 (dir. Eric Thompson; with Tom Courtenay as Leonard, Michael
 Robbins as Graham, Bridget Turner as Anna, Cheryl Kennedy as
 Joan, and Barry Andrews as Peter).
Television production: ATV, 18 May 1976 (dir. Caspar Wrede; cast as
 above, except Peter Egan as Peter).
Published: London: French, 1973.

The basic plot situation could hardly be simpler. Leonard, his sister Anna and Anna's husband, Graham, have just come home from their mother's funeral. Also present are Peter, one of Graham's employees, and Peter's girl-friend Joan. Graham fancies Joan, without getting anywhere very much; Leonard fancies Joan too, and by the end of the first act has got so far as to kiss her. In the second act some months have passed, and Joan is thinking of marriage with Leonard, but Leonard has not yet plucked up courage to tell Peter, a sporty type with, he keeps telling us, a ferocious temper. He never does, quite, and so in the end Joan decides that he doesn't want her enough and they drift apart ...

Some of my colleagues have chosen to take the play very seriously. Beneath the slight lyric grace, they find, is a tough reasonableness; though the play appears to be a comedy verging on farce, underneath it is a tragic study of man who does not want anything very much, whose almost total passivity is caused by a complete lack of desire, will or drive. I admire the intellectual enterprise of anyone who can get that much out of the play. I only wish I could. To me it seemed merely a flight of slightly whimsical fancy which failed to get up enough initial impetus to rise noticeably from the ground. Leonard is a character too soft and silly to be in any way attractive, and therefore his contracting-out of life — he is a graduate, like Jimmy Porter, who has chosen to work in a very menial capacity, in his case raking up leaves in the municipal parks and gardens — assumes little value as a gesture, while his habit of talking to himself or vaguely in the direction of anyone in earshot, whether they will listen or not (also a slightly Jimmy Porterish trait) lacks even the rhetorical elan which might make what he says interesting to us, if to no one on stage. Tom Courtenay plays him with a resourceful variety of slow-burns, absent-minded tics and looks of glassy incomprehension, and is sometimes very funny indeed.

John Russell Taylor, *Plays and Players*, Oct. 1972, p. 40-1

It's a very odd play really, odd for me. Anybody who has seen the two others might expect to see a fair old mess-up, people mistaking each other for each other's grandfathers — that sort of thing. This is about a sort of misfit in a rather conventional family who thinks he has fallen in love with a girl who thinks she has fallen in love with him; and neither of them have really, and he finishes up without her. How's that for a plot; it really isn't a story. Some people say the ending is sad, others say it's about how men can do perfectly well without women if they have to. I don't think it's about that. Some people *can* do without some people. This just happened to finish the way it did. One avoided the boy gets girl ending because it was dishonest, having worked a whole play about two people who are not destined to get together. The interesting thing about *Time and Time Again* is that I have upset the balance. The central character should be the driving force. I wanted to write a total vacuum, a central character who took no decisions, did nothing, everything was done for him and by simply taking no decisions he affects the whole course of the play. Doing nothing, he upsets about five lives. He comes through it in the most extraordinary way; everybody else ends up miserable. Like certain characters in life, he attracts people who have an irresistible impulse to push him in one direction, but he slides out of the push. Some people get angered by this type, others get concerned.

> Ayckbourn, 'The Joan Buck Interview',
> *Plays and Players*, Sept. 1972, p. 28-9

There's a terrible man in *Time and Time Again* called Graham, who is the monster bore of all time. He rambles on at great length. He was a wonderful man to speak and he got bigger and bigger when I was writing it. I had to cut it down a bit because one got his speech patterns going and one was able to talk as a Graham for hours on any topic.

> Ayckbourn, interviewed by Brian Connell,
> *The Times*, 5 Jan. 1976, p. 5

Time and Time Again I principally remember as the play in which I used water for the first time on stage. It wasn't , of course, the last. It was first produced in Scarborough in 1971, when the in-the-round company were still based at the Library Theatre in amongst the outsize books on the first floor. During the night, after a very happy opening performance, our modest pond leaked slowly through the stage into the Reading Room below, fusing the lights and wrecking the latest copies of *Gardeners' Weekly* and *Bellringers' World*. It was the play, some people observed, when the so-called 'darker' side of my writing started to emerge. Personally, I prefer to regard it as the play when I first began to attend to people as well as plot.

> Ayckbourn, programme note, Scarborough revival, Summer 1986

In much his best play so far, the result is rather as if Chekhov had decided to write a burlesque version of Dostoievsky's *The Idiot*, and the whole thing had been adapted to the middle-middle-class suburbs of some English provincial town. ... Is [Leonard] simply one of nature's victims, born to be put upon — to be bullied by his pupils, to find his wife in bed with another man, to be despised by his coarse brother-in-law, to be made a fool of when he decides to join in the football and

cricket, to be reduced to taking a job sweeping up leaves in the park?. ...
Is he not a man of some delicacy of temper, given to self-communing —
even if this does take the form of chatting up the gnome that sits fishing
in the garden pond — and a man of poetic leanings — even if his culture
does spring largely from having learnt the first lines of the poems in the
Oxford Book of English Verse — and to rueful self-mockery? Well, but
then is he not rather less one of nature's victims than one of nature's
victimizers, as he quietly demoralizes everybody he comes in contact
with, himself remaining totally unchanged?

> J.W. Lambert, 'Plays in Performance',
> *Drama*, Winter 1972, p. 15-16

In *Time and Time Again* Alan Ayckbourn for the first time pushed his
characters just beyond reality into that strange, off-key world of his own
creation, where people are viewed obliquely through his unique,
enigmatic vision. ... The virtuoso part is that of Graham (Leonard's
brother-in-law), a blustering, bullying dolt — a character Ayckbourn
uses in most of his plays as a sort of sounding board for the other
characters.

> Hazel Holt, 'Grasped the Essential Ayckbourn',
> *The Stage*, 27 May 1976, p. 15
> [of the television production]

Absurd Person Singular

Play in three acts.
First production: Library Th., Scarborough, 26 June 1972.
First London production: Criterion Th., 4 July 1973
  (dir. Eric Thompson; with Richard Briers as Sidney, Bridget Turner as
  Jane, Michael Aldridge as Ronald, Sheila Hancock as Marion,
  David Burke as Geoffrey, and Anna Calder-Marshal as Eva),
  transferred to Vaudeville Th.
First American production: Music Box. Th., 8 Oct. 1974
  (dir. Eric Thompson; with Richard Kiley as Ronald, Geraldine Page
  as Marion, and Sandy Dennis as Eva).
Television production: BBC-1, 1 Jan. 1985 (dir. Michael Simpson; with
  Nicky Henson as Sidney, Maureen Lipman as Jane, Geoffrey Palmer
  as Ronald, Prunella Scales as Marion, Michael Gambon as Geoffrey,
  and Cheryl Campbell as Eva).
Published; French; in *Three Plays* (Chatto and Windus, 1977; Penguin,
  1979).

The piece is enormously enjoyable as well as lethal in its portraits of six assorted middle-class English on three successive Christmas Eves. First we are in the speckless kitchen of Sidney and Jane; he a small tradesman, she an obsessive if muddle-headed housewife, entertaining their bank manager and his socially superior lady and a young architect and his difficult wife. Farcical disasters proliferate. So far, so good. Next we are in the progressive young architect's cluttered mess of a kitchen; his neurotic wife keeps attempting suicide, the bank manager's wife is floating out on a tide of alcohol, the visiting small tradesman's wife busies herself with cleaning up — and the curtain falls on a mood of still uproariously funny but increasingly chill hysteria as the sextet, in varying stages of collapse, join one by one in singing 'The Twelve Days of Christmas'. Last comes the big-house kitchen-sitting room of the bank manager, with some sort of an air of comfortable traditional values about it. But there is no heating, the bank manager's wife is upstairs, by now a hopeless alcoholic, he himself has withdrawn into a fog of affable indifference, the young architect's career has collapsed (though his suicidal wife has, all unexplained, turned into a briskly competent young woman). Enter the former small tradesman, now well on the way to big money as a property developer. With appalling geniality he sets the others, all too literally, dancing to his tune, and the play ends with a gruesomely funny demonstration of the power of money.

J.W. Lambert, 'Plays in Performance',
Drama, Autumn 1973, p. 20-1

I was becoming increasingly fascinated by the dramatic possibilities of offstage action. Not a new device, granted, but one with plenty of comic potential still waiting to be tapped. Very early on in my career as a dramatist I discovered that, given the chance, an audience's imagination can do far better work than any number of playwright's words. ... Thus, when I came to write *Absurd Person* and started by setting the action in Jane and Sidney Hopcraft's sitting room, I was halfway through the act before I realized that I was viewing the evening from totally the wrong perspective. Dick and Lottie were indeed monstrously overwhelming, hearty and ultimately very boring, and far better heard occasionally but not seen. By a simple switch of setting to the kitchen, the problem was

all but solved, adding incidentally far greater comic possibilities than the
sitting room ever held. For in this particular case, the obvious offstage
action was far more relevant than its on-stage counterpart. As a footnote:
since I was writing about parties and guests arriving, it also relieved me
of the tedium of all that hallo-how-are-you-good-bye-nice-to-see-you
business. *Absurd Person*, then, could be described as my first offstage
action play. It is also, some critics have observed, a rather weighty
comedy. Its last scene darkens considerably. I make no apologies for
this.

Ayckbourn, 'Preface', *Three Plays*, p. 7-8

[The first] act was perfect artifice, the skilled raconteur's bit. How were
we to get the guests, one by one and then in mixed doubles, into the
kitchen? And if there wasn't enough tonic water, how was Miss Shelley
to slip down to the corner deli in a rainstorm that would have dismayed
Noah? And if Mr. Blyden didn't want his upper-echelon guests to see
Miss Shelley in a raincoat and slouch hat that made her look like a
scruffy Cockney newsboy, how was he to conceal her except by locking
her out? The chess moves were immaculate, the pair were superb
farceurs capable of appearing and disappearing on metronome beat
(Mr. Blyden managed to send a bag of potato chips skyward while
precisely controlling the shape of its great flowering), and the spectacle
of the sodden Miss Shelley tapping piteously against the glass-panelled
back door like the Ghost of Christmas Drowned was just the lunatic,
logically-arrived-at cap the whole canny contrivance wanted. ... *Absurd
Person Singular* had one of the funniest second acts I have ever seen;
and death was the joke. ... [In the third act] the walls, the very lighting,
were pea green on this Christmas; artifice was over, hysteria was over,
the celebrants now needed to recoup from a joke grown near-dangerous.
... Laughter renewed itself in desperation; after all, that's where it had
come from, hadn't it? Mr. Ayckbourn's touch was light, his sympathies
warm, his vision the vision of a zoom lens: broad as a field when it was
time for a field day, pinpointed precisely when a lip twisted in wry
regret.

Walter Kerr, *Journey to the Center of the Theater* (New York, 1979),
p. 117-19 [on New York production]

Socially, *Absurd Person Singular* is an observant piece. The language, as
well as the furniture, places the characters with some precision. Marion's
use of the words 'enchanting', 'divine', and 'gorgeous' is nicely
contrasted with the Hopcrafts' lower-middle-class gentility: 'beg
pardon?' instead of 'sorry', 'the wife' instead of 'my wife', 'Ron' for
'Ronald' or 'Ronnie'. It is also very much a piece of its time. Sidney is

that success-symbol of the 1960s and early 1970s, the property speculator, complete with a suitably ugly philosophy about dog-eats-dog and you-scratch-my-back-I'll-scratch-yours. His rise is accompanied by the fall of those representing more traditional status, wealth, and power: Marion, the leisured gentlewoman, and Geoffrey, the educated professional who applies moral and aesthetic standards to his work. But it is rather more than a period chronicle, and also rather more than a sceptical study of marriage and relationships. It is about the change and decay to which we are all eventually subject. The Hopcrofts may have their temporary triumphs and the Evas their respites. The Geoffreys, Marions and Ronalds demonstrate a wider, more general truth. Like everything else in Ayckbourn's bleak, funny world, time itself is deeply inimical to hope, effort, fulfilment and happiness.

Benedict Nightingale, *An Introduction to Fifty Modern British Plays*, (London, 1982), p. 431-8

[Ayckbourn is] a political propagandist who works on people's minds without letting them know he's doing it or drawing attention to his own rectitude. He simply demonstrates, in terms audiences have to recognize as fact, the tragic absurdity of some of the things our society forces on human beings. Remember *Relatively Speaking* and all the fine-spun nonsense Ayckbourn wove out of a secretary coming down to spend the weekend at home with her boss and sleeping-partner? It was the technical skill I enjoyed then; but what's stuck in my mind is the image of one of that army of exploited, futureless office girls, slaves of London's air-conditioned harems, invading her nabob's Home County mini-dukery, with its croquet-lawn and three rhododendrons, and devastating it. Or remember *How the Other Half Loves*?. ... No one's written more sharply about the way class-politics express themselves as sexuality in Britain: the pull of upper-class women, wealth in its sexual form, on the competitive working-class meritocrat; the need for the educated wife to free herself from domestic bondage by inefficiency, as children have to free themselves from tutelage by adolescent untidiness. As much and more goes on beneath the technical polish of *Absurd Person Singular*. Formally, it's a sardonic parody of Dickens: Christmas Past, Christmas Present and Christmas Future, with Christmas Future bringing as its Santa Claus the wife-bullying property-developer of the first act, now a nosily confident regional tycoon whom both bank manager and architect need to flatter and defer to. The final scene, in which he forces them in their own stronghold to play the humiliating party-games they evaded at his party two years before, is as cuttingly vivid an image of the England of the Poulson affair as any British playwright is likely to offer us. It may not send anyone into Piccadilly to man the barricades, but I think it may make many of its audiences think twice before voting again for the free market economy, individual enterprise and the competitive principle.

Ronald Bryden, *Plays and Players*, Aug. 1973, p. 39-41

The Norman Conquests

Three related plays, each in two acts: *Table Manners* (originally entitled *Fancy Meeting You*), *Living Together* (originally entitled *Make Yourself at Home*), and *Round and Round the Garden.*
First production: Library Th., Scarborough, 18 June, 25 June, 9 July 1973 (dir. Ayckbourn).
First London production: Greenwich Th., 9 May, 21 May, 6 June 1974 (dir. Eric Thompson; with Tom Courtenay as Norman, Michael Gambon as Tom, Penelope Keith as Sarah, Felicity Kendal as Annie, Mark Kingston as Reg, and Penelope Wilton as Ruth); transferred to Globe Th., 1 Aug. 1974 (with Bridget Turner taking over as Ruth).
First New York production: Morosco Th., 1 Dec. 1975 (dir. Eric Thompson; with Richard Benjamin as Norman, Estelle Parsons as Sarah, and Carole Shelley as Ruth).
Television production: Thames, 5, 12 and 19 Oct. 1977 (dir. Herbert Wise; with Tom Conti as Norman, Penelope Keith as Sarah, Penelope Wilton as Annie, and Richard Briers as Reg).
Published: Chatto and Windus, 1975; Penguin, 1977.

A series of three plays about the same situation: an eventful family weekend at a country house, during which Norman, libertine and assistant librarian, makes advances toward his sister-in-law Annie, his other sister-in-law Sarah, and his wife Ruth. The plays occur not consecutively but simultaneously, 'one play' (as the director Eric Thompson says in a programme note) 'is the off stage of another': Table Manners *is set in the dining room,* Living Together *in the living room,* Round and Round the Garden *in the garden. ... As the play opens, Sarah and Reg are arriving at the home of the invalid mother of Annie, Reg and Ruth in order to relieve Annie who is about to go away on holiday and is planning a clandestine weekend with Norman. Her secret is forced out of her (a trifle too easily, I fear) by Sarah who forbids Annie to go. Exasperated, Norman chooses to*

30

remain at the house and within two days he has convinced Sarah to flee with him for a weekend soon, he has set up another, similar appointment with Annie, and he has seduced his own wife in the living room. (He has also succeeded, according to Round and Round the Garden, *in being rejected by them all at the very end). Between 5.30 p.m. Saturday and 9 a.m. Monday, we are offered a pleasing richness of comedy characterization, perceptively observed by Mr. Ayckbourn, lucid, intelligent and funny.*

Perry Pontac, *Plays and Players*, July 1974, p. 42-3

Since we could only afford six actors, they should have that number of characters. ... Ideally they should only have two stage entrances since that's the way our temporary Library Theatre set-up is arranged (but then this is common to all my plays). There were other minor pre-conditions peculiar to this venture. The actor I had in mind to play Norman coundn't join us for the first few days of the season — which necessitated him making a late first entrance in one of the plays (*Table Manners*) to facilitate rehearsals. If this all makes me sound like a writer who performs to order, I suppose it's true. I thrive when working under a series of pre-conditions, preferably when they are pre-conditions over which I have total control. ... I decided in the case of *The Norman Conquests* to write them crosswise. That is to say, I started with Scene One of *Round and Round the Garden*, then the Scene One's of the other two plays and so on through the Scene Two's. It was an odd experience writing them, rather similar to Norman's own in fact. I found myself grappling with triplet sisters all with very different personalities. Climaxes, comic ones naturally, seemed to abound everywhere. Hardly had I finished dealing with the fury of Reg's game (*Living Together*) than I was encountering a frenzied Sarah trying to seat her guests (*Table Manners*) or Ruth beating off the advances of an uncharacteristically amorous Tom (*Round and Round the Garden*). Strangely too, each play, although dealing with the same characters and events, began to develop a distinct atmosphere of its own. *Table Manners* was the most robust and, as it proved on stage, the most overtly funny. *Round and Round the Garden*, possibly due to its exterior setting, took a more casual and (as it contains the beginning and the end of the cycle) a more conventional shape. *Living Together* has a tempo far slower than anything I had written before and encouraged me, possibly because of the sheer over-all volume of writing involved, to slacken the pace in a way I had never dared to do in any comedy.

Ayckbourn, 'Preface', p. 10-12

Meals are convenient times when people are willy nilly forced to sit opposite each other and possibly exchange conversation. ... There's always somebody in my plays — well, not always, but often — who wants to do things properly, according to the way they think they ought to do it. In *The Normans*, Sarah's attempt to have an embassy banquet in that naff house, with only lettuce in the fridge — it serves her right, really. ... She fancies Norman more than any of them, so she's fighting herself, and she's also fighting the sins of her sisters-in law. She's really trying to touch a safe base; and the safe base is rolled napkins, and knives and forks, and man-woman-man-woman, and 'Hasn't it been a lovely day?'

Ayckbourn, *Conversations*, p. 116

What, though, does this final study of a grisly family weekend in Sussex tell us of Ayckbourn's overall purpose? It suggests, in part, the plays are a study of the loneliness of the long-distance egoist with Tom Courtenay's suburban Don Juan finally exposed as a man driven, not so much by lust as by the constant itch for attention. It also suggests Ayckbourn is striking a small, defiant blow for men's lib urging the weaker, masculine sex to come out from behind the kitchen sink and get back to the garden deck-chairs where they belong: Ayckbourn is no shrill anti-feminist, but he does imply that, at a certain level of bourgeois life, men are reduced to gutless salary slaves driven on by Brunhildes in pearls. And finally the plays are about the Ibsenite stranglehold of the past in that the bedridden, once-promiscuous mother upstairs has clearly stunted the sex-lives of her three progeny. In short, like all good comedy, the plays are about something important.

Michael Billington, *The Guardian*, 29 May 1974

The Norman Conquests is not only funny but impossibly wise about sex, marriage, love and loneliness. ... What makes *The Norman Conquests* memorable is not Ayckbourn's cleverness so much as his compassion. As Norman's strategies start to fail, the consequences seem almost tragic. We realize that Ayckbourn's characters can never fulfil even their modest dreams of adventure and romance; they are doomed by circumstance and social convention to a defeated middle age. Perhaps the fate of the six is foreshadowed by Ayckbourn's seventh and unseen character: a family matriarch who never leaves her bedroom because she 'just has no desire to get up'.

Frank Rich, 'Ménage à Six', *Time*, 19 June 1978, p. 49
[on television version]

The world Ayckbourn here creates is the same as that inhabited by the Gambols, dependent on corner-of-the-eye recognition of character, situation, lines, development and mores. The married couple, Sarah and Reg, might have been dramatizations of Gaye and George. ... Norman has the lines — he calls himself 'a gigolo trapped in a haystack' — and he gets the action. The others, threatened to various degrees, retreat into character or pathological variations thereon. Now this sort of writing, I would hazard, needs sustained bravura to work. But Ayckbourn denies Norman real targets and dissipates his energies by adhering to (what seems so far) a footling scheme. And the sustained energy has gone into the role of Sarah. ... Sarah announces that they must leave early for home because her cleaning woman is coming and she, Sarah, must have time to clean the house before she comes. This is a Gambols joke of immense calculation and no dramatic credibility, rootless and indulgent.

W. Stephen Gilbert, *Plays and Players*, June 1974, p. 44

See also:
John Elsom, ed., *Post-War British Theatre Criticism* (London, 1981), p. 233-40.
Gareth and Barbara Lloyd Evans, eds., *Plays in Review, 1956-1980* (London, 1985), p. 202-8.
B.A. Young, *The Mirror up to Nature* (London, 1982), p. 92-6.

Absent Friends

A play in two acts.
First production: Library Th., Scarborough, 17 June 1974.
First London production: Garrick Th., 23 July 1975
(dir. Eric Thompson; with Richard Briers as Colin, Peter Bowles as Paul, and Pat Heywood as Diana).
First American production: Kennedy Centre, Washington, 11 July 1977
(dir. Eric Thompson; with Eli Wallach as Colin, and Anne Jackson as Diana).
Television production: BBC-2, 29 Sept. 1985 (dir. Michael Simpson; with Tom Courtenay as Colin, Dinsdale Landen as Paul, Julia McKenzie as Diana, and Maureen Lipman as Marge).
Published: in *Three Plays* (Chattto and Windus, 1977; Penguin, 1979); French, 1975.

Absent Friends *is placed firmly in the heart of the Ayckbourn country; Derek Cousins has designed an appalling summary of young-middle-aged businessman's provincial chic, all brick, pickled wood and prints of vintage cars, stunned by a bright lime-green three-piece suite. It belongs to Paul, a cranky bully, and Diana, a lachrymose Hausfrau. Also present are John, a feebly vivacious dud, and his wife Evelyn, a bejeaned sexpot slut, gum-chewing sulkily over her baby's pram, and Marg, all angular exuberance and contemptuous concern for the outsize baby of a husband she has left ill at home, and whose frequent telephone callls provide a rather effortful running gag. They have gathered, more or less reluctantly, to offer tea and sympathy to Colin, a former friend, returning on a brief visit soon after the loss of his fiancée by drowning. In the event he turns out to be in a state of irrepressible euphoria, armed with happy memories, a photograph album ('Oh, she is lovely ... wasn't she!'), and quite content with the company of his intended in-laws; and when his old friends' gauche attempts at sympathy have finally been disposed of he no less cheerfully sets about telling them what's wrong with their own lives. ... [Ayckbourn] draws his crew of provincial-suburban small fry with a truth which compels us to see their littleness but also enables us to feel for them, never forces us into the position of self-consciously superior voyeurs.*

J.W. Lambert, 'Plays in Performance', *Drama*, Autumn 1975, p. 42

In Scarborough, I was very nervous of the play on the first night. I said to the cast, 'Look, I just don't know what's going to happen with this one; the audience may not laugh from beginning to end because, for the first time, we're deliberately asking them not to do so'. ... Because of the intimacy of the theatre up there and the ability of the audience to lean in on the play, it became a sort of keyhole experience. ... The tensions had been there and, in a sense, one is prepared for such events [as Diana's hysterical second act outburst] by the presence, in the middle, of the awful Colin slowly accelerating any imminent crisis with his platitudes and words of goodwill. Colin has gained this immunity through having been touched by tragedy. He's like a man you've always detested being suddenly struck with an incurable disease; as everyone knows he only has six months to live, gestures of courtesy and tolerance are offered when, in normal circumstances, a fourpenny one would have been forthcoming. Colin's immunity is something he doesn't really deserve. ... I have great sympathy for people like Diana in *Absent*

Friends, desperately trying to make a marriage work. The women in this latest play, in fact, are probably drawn more sympathetically than the men. And that puts the record straight, because most plays about marriage tend to get written from the man's point of view.

Ayckbourn, interviewed by Michael Coveney, 'Scarborough Fare',
Plays and Players, Sept. 1975, p. 16-17, 19

The play is an unmitigated failure. The actors are compelled by the absence of genuinely funny dialogue and inadequate characterization to over-act in the same way that the set overstates. High points of wit include Evelyn's verdict on Paul's virility: like being made love to by a 'clammy bag of cement'. Colin, vying for the joke-of-the-month, describes Marg's overweight husband as 'a polythene bag full of water. There is a limit to how funny unfunny people can be, and Alan Ayckbourn has overstepped it in this play. His actors are left to huff and puff and bring the house down. It stays firmly up, unshaken by a tremor.

Craig Raine, 'Fair Play', *New Statesman*, 1 Aug. 1975, p. 152

Absent Friends ... is about the nature of happiness, and the effect which contact with happiness has upon the discontented and unhappy. It is Mr. Ayckbourn's finest play, and if it is the saddest and most moving thing that he has written, it is also the most clear-sighted and the funniest. It makes greater demands on the emotional maturity and perceptiveness of its audience than any of Mr. Ayckbourn's previous work. In Eric Thompson's production it makes them slowly and deliberately. Perhaps not all audiences will be able to respond to them fully. But those that can will leave the theatre having heard the real, true music of humanity, and with their lives enriched. ... The play disturbs as well as illuminates, and there are two greatly effective incidents in the second act — when Miss Heywood makes a remarkable speech about the Royal Canadian Mounted Police, and again when in exasperation she pours cream over her husband's head — that are not easy to reconcile with the theory of a beneficent universe. ... In its ending it is properly indeterminate. One character, Marg, is possibly influenced for good. One cannot be certain, but there is a margin of probability. Another, John, at least has his eyes opened, and admits to it in a speech which Mr. Brooks delivers with a convincing, flippant bitterness. It is on Diana and Paul that Colin's impact has been greatest and perhaps (who knows?) disastrous. After the hysteria of the two incidents I have mentioned they are left bemused and exhausted, which may, or may not, be the same as exorcised.

Harold Hobson, 'Uneasy Partnerships',
Sunday Times, 27 July 1975

The play is like a comic inversion of *The Wild Duck* with Colin as the suburban Gregers Werle who, in trying to do good, wreaks untold havoc. I find this character horribly believable and funny: particularly as embodied by the marvellous Richard Briers, mouth permanently agape like a hungry sea-lion, fist constantly jabbing people in the shoulder in proof of fellow-feeling. And, as always in Ayckbourn, there is a melancholic sub-text about the miseries of small-town life in which nervy businessmen offer up their wives in order to keep the vital contract and in which talented would-be athletes end up as broken-down fire prevention officers. What the play lacks, however, is that element of sheer surprise that keeps Ayckbourn's best comedies frothing and bubbling: once you've realized that Colin is a beaming, innocent catalyst then you can safely predict the collapses into rancorous hysteria that his toothy presence invites.

Michael Billington, *The Guardian*, 24 July 1975

Confusions

Five short one-act plays, to be performed together.
First production: Library Th., Scarborough, 30 Sept. 1974
(dir. Ayckbourn).
First London production: Apollo Th., 19 May 1976 (dir. Alan Strachan; with Pauline Collins as Lucy, Paula, Milly and Beryl; John Alderton as Harry, Waiter, Gosforth and Arthur; Sheila Gish as Rosemary, Bernice, Mrs. Pearce and Doreen; Derek Fowlds as Terry, Martin, Stewart and Ernest; James Cossins as Waiter, Pearce, Vicar and Charles).
First American production: Body Politic Th., Chicago, Spring 1982.
Published: French,1977; Methuen Student Edition, ed. Russell Whiteley, 1983.

In the first sketch a harassed young mother, apparently abandoned by her husband, puts in their pathetically suburban place a nosy couple from next door who wants to know what has been going on. They never find out. Nor do we. But the way in which their hostess brusquely dismisses them, in terms which would literally suit the nursery, is a sharp lesson in the art of social condescension. Then we are treated to the sight of a commercial traveller (perhaps the defecting husband from the previous sketch) trying to pick up a young woman in a provincial hotel lounge. He is up to no good as he toys with his room keys; and she is well aware of his motives. His chatter and eagerness to ply her with drink are interrupted by the arrival of her much more guarded girl friend. And so to bed? Well, you had better wait and see. Thence anyhow to a restaurant where two couples are separately discovered dining without much pleasure. ... His types are always true to themselves. This comes out vividly in a village fete to which Mr. Ayckbourn next invites us. Everything goes increasingly wrong (especially a confession of pregnancy, inadvertently broadcast round the grounds); and in the final interlude there is a circle of park benches whose shifting occupants bore one another in grisly rotation.

Eric Shorter, 'Regions', *Drama*, Winter 1974, p. 65-6

The last confusion is actually quite Beckettian; a cast of five telling one another their troubles and realizing that 'you might as well be talking to yourself'. This is the kind of thing Mr. Ayckbourn does least well. ... In another piece, John Alderton, a travelling salesman, proceeds with great speed and smoothness from affability to desperation in his efforts to seduce Pauline Collins and Sheila Gish, two travelling salesgirls. This is Mr. Ayckbourn's best dark piece to date; all three characters are naturals for the urns.

Robert Cushman, *The Observer*, 23 May 1976

Confusions — the title — is one of the few things wrong with this collection of five short plays. They're concerned more with separation, obsession and isolation. ... If you want to find them, there are threads and echoes between the individual short plays, but they are not important. ... In 'Between Mouthfuls' Mr. Cossins's foodless, wordless gobbling as a business man in a restaurant is the glass of fascism, the mould of formality gone berserk. His fury at the menu, the wine list, the bottle of wine, the presence of the waiter, the absence of the waiter, his wife, his *life* becomes a joy. His eyes come closer together; his jowls move as if in slow motion beneath the scrutiny of a magnifying lens. He is irritation incarnate. We recognize him.

Julian Jebb, *Plays and Players*, July 1976, p. 24-5

I recalled a sketch I had written for an entertainment presented in Horsham for a week by Oscar Quitak before it faded into oblivion (the show, *Mixed Blessings*, was intended as a sequel to *Mixed Doubles*). Being mean like most writers, I snatched the piece back and wrote four accompanying pieces specifically for the five actors I'd got in the company. The idea was to show off their talents (there are about 23 parts in all), and it was also a chance to work in the one-act medium.

Ayckbourn, interviewed by Michael Coveney, 'Scarborough Fare',
Plays and Players, Sept. 1975, p. 17

Jeeves

Musical. Book and lyrics by Ayckbourn, music by Andrew Lloyd Webber, based on the Jeeves stories by P.G. Wodehouse, mainly *The Code of the Woosters*.
First London production: Her Majesty's Th., 22 Apr. 1975
(dir. Eric Thompson; with David Hemmings as Bertie Wooster, and Michael Aldridge as Jeeves).
Unpublished; original cast recording issued by MCA (MCF 2726).

It was a small, extremely resourceful and witty adaptation of Wodehouse to the stage, partly torpedoed by an uneven score and a theatre four times too large for it. ... Most of what is right about Jeeves is Alan Ayckbourn's book, the most literate and genuinely witty a British musical comedy has offered since Sandy Wilson's *Valmouth*. Ayckbourn has grasped the essence of Wodehouse's comedy: the way his swift, curlicued dramatic monologues, strewn with fractured quotation and embroidered cliché, counterpoint and sophisticate the old-fashioned farce plots and characters he borrowed from 1920s musical comedy. ... Ayckbourn wisely makes Jeeves a musical comedy narrated by Bertie Wooster, in one of his misguided attempts at village hall entertainment, with occasional assistance and correction from his peerless valet, mentor and Machiavel of the title. This has the virtue of preserving most of the best jokes, descriptive rather than conversational. ... What goes wrong, chiefly, is Andrew Lloyd Webber's score.

Ronald Bryden, *Plays and Players*, July 1975, p. 28

The show was still running [at the Bristol try-out] at the dangerous length of four hours, and morale was low. David Hemmings, who really held the company together, was extremely pessimistic. ... Unfortunately there was panic after that and the cuts made were drastic, involving the virtual elimination of one of our more distinguished actresses, and some of the better parts of the show. It was a situation the producer most fears, big musical thundering toward the West End like a train that cannot be stopped for long enough for drastic repairs. ... Doing eight shows a week while trying to work in rewrites is the wrong way to prepare for the West End opening. As with many musicals that go wrong in this way, by the time we got to London the company had had so many changes and had worked so hard that the actors were in a state of complete exhaustion — in particular David. I watched the faces of people coming out after one of the charity previews at Her Majesty's. They were in a state of disbelief. The first night was a disaster.

Michael White [producer], *Empty Seats* (London, 1984), p. 136-7

Bedroom Farce

A play in two acts.
First production: Library Th., Scarborough, 16 June 1975
    (dir. Ayckbourn).
First London production: Lyttelton Th., 14 March 1977 (dir. Peter Hall
    and Ayckbourn; with Stephen Moore as Trevor, Maria Aitken as
    Susannah, Michael Gough as Ernest, and Joan Hickson as Delia),
    transferred to Prince of Wales Th.
First New York production: Brooks Atkinson Th., 29 Mar. 1979
    (dir. Peter Hall and Ayckbourn; with six members of London cast).
Television production: ITV, 28 Sept. 1980.
Published: French; *Three Plays* (Chatto and Windus, 1977;
    Penguin, 1979).

The first bedroom — and to my mind the funniest — is occupied by an ageing pair, Delia and Ernest, who are celebrating their wedding anniversary , the second by Malcolm and Kate, who are giving a house-warming party, and the third by Nick and Jan, who are friends of Malcolm and Kate, Jan also being an old flame of Delia and Ernest's son, Trevor. It is the fourth couple, Trevor and his wife Susannah, who cause all the fuss on this particular night and end up, ambiguously, in Malcolm and Kate's bed. But a bare outline of the plot gives very little idea of the ludicrous and yet always quite credible predicaments into which Mr. Ayckbourn manoeuvres this octet. Highlights for me were Nick, who is confined to bed with a strained back, attempting to retrieve a book and ending up immobile on the floor, Malcolm, a do-it-yourself enthusiast, constructing a 'surprise' piece of furniture for his wife at three a.m., and, best of all, Ernest and Delia, retiring to bed for pilchards on toast and a reading of Tom Brown's Schooldays. *The cast is uniformly excellent, but these two — he the incarnation of a Thurber-esque downtrodden husband and she the sort of lady whose instinctive reaction to her daughter-in-law's desperate plea for help in her sex life is to offer her a cup of tea — show particular accomplishment.*

Sandy Wilson, *Plays and Players*, May 1977, p. 24-5

Comedy, I read somewhere, consists of larger than life characters in real situations. Farce, on the other hand, portrays real characters projected into incredible situations. *Bedroom Farce* is a comedy about real characters who, projected into incredible situations, start behaving in a larger than life manner as the situations appear to them too horribly real.

Ayckbourn, interview in National Theatre programme

I never really liked *Bedroom Farce* very much. Yes, I did: I got to like it quite a lot. I felt rather extraordinary when I wrote it, though: I didn't quite know why I'd written it. It was very strange. It cropped up in the middle of my serious phase: this rather jolly play suddenly arrived. And I think I was rather rude to it. I said to it: 'I'm an *Absent Friends* man now, a much more serious dramatist.'

Ayckbourn, *Conversations*, p. 113

Three beds face us. They are respectively heavy old-fashioned walnut with legs; genteel and candlewicked divan; spotlit duvet-style in front of louvre-door wardrobe. Instantly, we have the characters outlined; elderly old-fashioned, contented lower-middle, aspiring modern. ... The economy with which Mr. Ayckbourn delineates character signifies skill of an exceptionally high order. Of the elderly pair, for instance, we know that their idea of a happy day is one which ends with sardines on toast in bed (they discuss with fitting gravity the crisis of a sardineless larder and the acceptability of pilchards as a substitute), and that is about all we do know; yet — this is where the skill comes in — we feel they live next door, so acute is the author's selection of what is truly representative.

Bernard Levin, *Sunday Times*, 20 Mar. 1977

The boudoir ceases to be, as traditionally in bedroom farce, the locus of illicit sexual mischief, and becomes instead the place where licit relationships are most sorely tested. Yet neither relationships nor tests are of a particularly sexual sort; the hotbed of errant eroticism has become the cold bed of marriages settled into routine and gamesmanship that can all too easily be disrupted by the most inconsequential turmoil from without. The bedroom, then, as the soft but not especially lusty underbelly of everyday conjugality: resigned on the left, edgily witty on the right, and coyly playful in the middle — all strategies meant to mask the naked unease exhibited by Trevor and Susannah's portable and contagious bed of pain. Yet the old couple are viewed more positively than the younger ones — perhaps because they hark back to a less sex-tormented era — and their use of the bedroom as a conversation pit for reviewing the day's trivia comes across as a sensible, though Pyrrhic, victory. Consider Delia, who, exuding equanimity, tells her distraught daughter-in-law, 'My mother used to say: if s-e-x ever rears its ugly head, close your eyes before you see the rest of it'. That remark is typical of Ayckbourn's people: It is, like them, both silly and wise. ... The way a bit of physical space is filled or a bit of conversational space is left empty is calculated to provide maximum hilarity, but the calculation always wears the happy disguise of absolute spontaneity.

John Simon, 'From Top to Botho', *New York*, 16 Apr. 1979, p. 88

Of course, it's full of sex, but sex of a different sort. It covers a whole wide range of sexual troubles, sexual problems. ... [Trevor and Susannah] are two totally incompatible people, friends I hope we will all recognize if not wish upon ourselves. They're the sort of people who think that everything has happened only to them. They can't imagine that anyone else has problems. They are wildly selfish egoists, both of them.

Ayckbourn, quoted by Benedict Nightingale,
'Ayckbourn — Comic Laureate of Britain's Middle Class',
New York Times, 25 Mar. 1979, Sec. II, p. 1, 4

[Ayckbourn] told me that the play had been announced and publicized as the centre of the new Scarborough season even before it was written. It was due to rehearse on a Monday; he started writing it on the previous Wednesday, wrote all day Wednesday and most of the night, all day Thursday and most of the night, all day Friday and most of the night; on Saturday he typed it out, and on Sunday armed with some duplicated copies he drove up to Scarborough. He gave it to the cast on Monday morning, and after the reading collapsed in bed for two days. He said this was the kind of pressure he needed, and usually induced, to write a play. ...

There's nothing sadder than playing uproarious comedy. There can be no emotional release. The satisfaction is manipulative rather than

41

sharing a feeling. Albert Finney once told me he feels frustrated at the end of a farce, but elevated and high at the end of a tragedy. It's a particular problem with this play. The laughs are enormous and continuous, yet if any actor actually plays a laugh, or encourages one by even a lift of the eyebrow, the whole structure collapses. ...

[The company] have grown, inevitably, to think more and more of it as a series of laughs. But it is also about the fact that if you give yourself to somebody you are vulnerable. So it's safer not to give, but you are then lonely and unhappy. ...

[The company] were utterly miserable, as usual. I've never known a more paranoid group. Perhaps it's because to play Ayckbourn properly you have to dig deep, be serious, and then get laughed at. It wounds the personality.

Peter Hall [co-director], *Diaries* (London, 1983),
p. 174-75, 285-86, 409-10, 432-33

Just Between Ourselves

A play in two acts.
First production: Library Th., Scarborough, 28 Jan. 1976
  (dir. Ayckbourn).
First London production: Queen's Th., 20 Apr. 1977
  (dir. Alan Strachan; with Colin Blakely as Dennis, Rosemary Leach
  as Vera, Michael Gambon as Neil, Stephanie Turner as Pam, and
  Constance Chapman as Marjorie).
Television production: ITV, 23 July 1978 (dir. Marc Miller; with
  Richard Briers as Dennis, Rosemary Leach as Vera, Stephen Moore
  as Neil, Rosemary McHale as Pam, and Constance Chapman as
  Marjorie).
First American production; McCarter Th. Co., Princeton, N.J.,
  30 Sept. 1981.
Published: French, 1978; in *Joking Apart and other Plays* (Chatto and
  Windus, 1979; Penguin, 1982); in *Plays of the Seventies*,
  ed. Roger Cornish and Violet Ketels (Methuen, 1986).

The settings for Mr. Ayckbourn's plays have roamed through every room in the suburban semi-detached — where can he go next? Where else but the garage? And at the centre of Helga Wood's carefully cluttered set [at Scarborough], taking up most of the acting area, is an ageing (F registered) Morris Minor

1000. Dennis, the jovial bluff know-all, is selling his wife's car because she's been having trouble with her nerves. Diffident Neil is sort of thinking of buying it for his wife because she's — erm — lacking fulfilment. Just Between Ourselves *is, on the surface, one of the lightest, slightest of Alan Ayckbourn's plays. For the first half the dialogue rarely rises above that level of superficial banal non-communication that passes for conversation in suburbia. ... Yet when the sharp edges show through — like broken teeth in soft gums, the depths of the subtexts are as black as Beckett or Bond. Take that awesome symbol of the old banger. The engine hasn't been turned over for months — and anyway the garage door is jammed. Where the manic black comedy of* Absent Friends *dealt with death and our refusal to recognize it, this play is about growing old — an even more sombre theme because you can't ignore it. Each of the four scenes takes place on someone's birthday. Each of the five characters deals with the problem differently. Neil accepts it as he does all the other disasters life deals him; his wife Pam is fighting the fear that she's no longer attractive, useful, wanted, loved; Dennis laughs it off, like all life's little difficulties that he can't cope with; his mother Marjorie relishes the fretting and the worry; and his wife Vera eventually and inevitably succumbs. But Alan Ayckbourn's reaction to cosmic gloom is, quite properly, a high pitched shriek of nervous laughter, and the play has one moment of elegantly contrived comic absurdity that must go down as a classic of British farce. Dennis is struggling in the car with a half-undressed Pam while his wife is chasing his mother round the garage with an electric drill; Neil comes in carrying a birthday cake covered with lighted candles and turns on the fairy lights with a fatuous grin.*

Robin Thornber, *The Guardian*, 30 Jan. 1976

Just Between Ourselves, *Ten Times Table* and *Joking Apart* could be described as the first of my 'winter' plays. ... To encourage and develop our much needed winter audience, I launched my latest play, *Just Between Ourselves*, at a time when it would, we hoped, do the most good at the box office. At the same time, the pressure that had always been on me to produce a play suited primarily to a holiday audience was no longer there. ... The result was a rather sad (some say a rather savage) play with themes concerned with total lack of understanding, with growing old and with spiritual and mental collapse. Dennis, the husband, is no calculating villain. Nor is he, I contend, particularly unusual. Just a man pathologically incapable of understanding beyond a certain level. His wife's cries for help go unanswered not because he ignores them or fails to hear them but because he honestly hasn't the slightest idea what they're about. The wife, Vera, hampered by a lack of ability to express herself clearly or maybe too inhibited to do so, sufferers from a conventional upbringing that has taught her that the odds on her being wrong and her husband being right are high. Slowly, the last vestiges of self-confidence are drained from her. Vera sits empty, huddled and withdrawn in the garden, unwilling to go back into a house that is no longer hers. ... It continued my small progress, first started in *Absent Friends*, towards my unattainable goal: to write a totally effortless, totally truthful, unforced comedy shaped like a flawless diamond in which one can see a million reflections, both one's own and other people's.

Ayckbourn, 'Preface', Joking Apart and Other Plays

I never sit down to write a grim play. Vera in *Just Between* took me by surprise. I was going to write about a man who was awfully nice and friendly and whom everyone loathed — there is a strange breed like that. But out of the corner of my eye I saw this wife, she just came in with a cup of tea to start with, and she was *crumbling away*. And I thought, hang on, what's happening to *her*?

Ayckbourn, quoted by Anthony Masters,
'The Essentially Ambiguous Response',
The Times, 4 Feb. 1981, p. 8

This is the *Otherwise Engaged* [by Simon Gray] of the lower middle class male who, like Dennis, seeks refuge in his fake handyman's garage or, like Neil, in hypochondria. Ayckbourn offers no redeeming qualities to these men. ... The trouble is that Ayckbourn's minimalist, self-consciously elegant form creates only collections of behaviour, and omits the messy bits that might blur the outline but bear some resemblance to people. If his play tells of a whimper, it tells it by a whimper.

Victoria Radin, 'Small Rooms — Open Spaces',
The Observer, 24 Apr. 1977, p. 26

His technique, so brilliantly successful in farce, is inappropriate for his subject. Ayckbourn tries to hold this play together, as is his wont, by parallelism and symmetry. There are four scenes, each with different birthdays; and in each scene, Dennis tries to sell Vera's car to Neil and Pam, dropping a little in price each time, until by the year's end, he is giving it away. This formal pattern is useful for farces like *The Norman Conquests*: Ayckbourn can play around with expectations of his audience. But in *Just Between Ourselves*, the design is obtrusive and apparently at a tangent to the play's meaning. The non-selling of the car does not reflect on the growing unhappiness of the characters; and the climax of the third scene, a chaotic birthday surprise arranged by Dennis which goes wrong, seems just contrived. The formal structure interfered with the unfolding of the plot.

John Elsom, 'Telling Tales', *The Listener*, 28 Apr. 1977, p. 566

It is not even a black comedy, but a bitter depiction of real people in real pain, and in it Mr. Ayckbourn has, with considerable courage, crossed a gulf wide enough to make even the best of his earlier work almost invisible on the farther shore. ... The verdict must be that with this play Mr. Ayckbourn has grown up. ... Much of Mr. Ayckbourn's usual dramatic furniture is on show; at one level he is still in a world in which the man who has been medically forbidden sugar in his tea inevitably gets it, and in which vital conversations are drowned by the relentless blackanddeckering of the obsessive handyman. And his observation is as acute as ever, as when the indiscreet mother-in-law, urgently hushed when she starts to say what she should not, complies, at any rate to her own satisfaction, by lowering her voice and saying it again in a piercing *sotto voce*. But the author has other fish to fry this time, and the hell in which his fish are sizzling is at times so convincing that I found I had to look away from the stage in pain. Alan Ayckbourn has gained an immense reputation with a series of plays in which puppets dance most divertingly on their strings. Here he has cut the strings and then stuck the knife into the puppets. They bleed.

Bernard Levin, 'Mr. Ayckbourn Changes Trains', *Sunday Times*, 24 Apr. 1977

Ayckbourn's greatest gift is a sort of innocence. His astonishing skills at manipulating stage business (his use of props is equalled only by Osborne), his dead accurate ear, can distract us from what amounts to a visionary picture of English middle-class life. There is neither sentimentality nor censoriousness in this play. It does not seem in the least inappropriate to evoke Chekhov when writing about him. Like the master, he sees life as it is — and life as it ought to be.

Julian Jebb, *Plays and Players*, June 1977, p. 28

Ten Times Table

A play in two acts
First production: Stephen Joseph Th., Scarborough, 18 Jan. 1977.
First London production: Globe Th., 5 Apr. 1978 (dir. Ayckbourn; with
    Paul Eddington as Ray, and Julia McKenzie as Helen).
Published; French, 1978; in *Joking Apart and Other Plays* (Chatto and
    Windus, 1979; Penguin, 1982).

*The table in question is a committee table, situated in a yawning
hotel ballroom in the north country town of Pendon. Ten ill-
assorted locals spend half-a-year in and out of this drafty venue,
organizing a folk pageant to commemorate the Massacre of the
Pendon Twelve, a misty eighteenth-century tale of militant
agriculturalists mown down by an unfeeling militia. Compared
to their illustrious predecessors, this present-day Pendon Ten
are very deeply divided. The committee chairman wants the
pageant to arouse the town's flagging community spirit. A sub-
committee of committed subversives is determined to rewrite
Pendon's gory glory as an unequivocal triumph of the Left.
There is also a right-wing splinter committee, keener to re-enact
history than to rewrite it — even to the point of splintering
Leftist skulls over the market-place cobbles. In his plot line, at
least, Ayckbourn has made a sharp move to pastures northern
and new. The politics of Pendon are a long way from those cosy
domestic holocausts of south-eastern suburbia. Yet the faithful
need not altogether fear. Apart from the extremist chiefs, Tim, a
haut-Yorkshire, mad-militarist, dog breeder, and Eric, a bas-
Lancashire Marxist, the characters are all refugees from the
master's more conventional comedies. ...*

Ayckbourn's compulsory incommunicants are Philippa, the
whispering wife of Eric, and Lawrence, a maudling alcoholic, pickled
stiff from tongue-to-toe. To complete the comic machinery comes the
committee's ancient secretary who is all too keen to communicate but is
deaf and totally incommunicado to everything but the suggestion of a
drink. Ayckbourn fully exploits this and every other humorous
possibility within the creaking fabric of the hotel, from the erratic disco-
lights of the ballroom stage to the persistent carpet bashers in the first
floor bedroom. ... The truest-to-life creation is the character of Donald,
the pedantic councillor, obsessed by commas and protocol, one of the

world's million committee men who promise to bring pressure to bear, to clear the channels, etcetera, etcetera, but in the end can get not a penny from the council grants committee nor even police permission to ride a horse up the High Street.

Peter Stothard, *Plays and Players*, June 1978, p. 30

Undoubtedly draws for its subject matter on experiences gained during 1976. We were due in October of that year to transfer from our present theatre home, the first floor of the Scarborough Public Library, to our new temporary housing, the far more commodious ground floor of the old Boys' Grammar School. For me, this entailed attending an interminable series of repetitive (and largely non-productive) committee meetings to finance and facilitate the move. Up till then, I had had little to do with committees. Little by little, their procedures and protocols began to intrigue me. And particularly the people involved and the way they used these procedures. ... *Ten Times Table* is a study of the committee person. It breaks a pattern for me in that I leave my usually domestic setting for the more public surroundings of the ballroom of the quite awful Swan Hotel, where everyone at some times must have stayed, much against their better judgement. The play could be described, I suppose, as a predominantly sedentary farce with faintly allegorical overtones. In more innocent days, it would probably have been sub-titled a romp.

Ayckbourn, 'Preface', *Joking Apart and Other Plays*, p. 8

Directing his own work for the first time in London, Ayckbourn has urged his company into a brilliant technical display of matter over mind, so that in the speed of the quarrels and the ultimate technical debacle we manage to lose sight of the fact that this is really a play about remarkably little.

Sheridan Morley, *Shooting Stars* (London, 1983), p. 129
[reprinted from *Punch*]

It doesn't explore the seam of anguish Ayckbourn mined in *Just Between Ourselves* nor does it have the technical brilliance of *Bedroom Farce*, but it is still, by West End standards, a very funny play. What it also shows is Ayckbourn's ability to build up a portrait of a community through the interstices of the plot.

Michael Billington, *The Guardian*, 6 Apr. 1978

No one writing comedy today has a finer ear for the dotty logic of conversational small change or the hideous animosities and resentments that can lurk behind slack, blank English faces. He is at his best drawing deceptively mundane portraits of dull people with vivid ambitions. ... It is England writ small by a cool and caustic chronicler of large frustrations in small places. It is also hugely funny: not because these people are witty but because they are drawn with a sense of conspiratorial glee.

John Peter, Sunday Times, 16 Apr. 1978, p. 37

Joking Apart

A play in two acts.

First production: Stephen Joseph Th., Scarborough, 11 Jan. 1978 (dir. Ayckbourn).

First London production: Globe Th., 7 Mar. 1979 (dir. Ayckbourn; with Christopher Cazenove as Richard and Alison Steadman as Anthea).

Published: in *Joking Apart and Other Plays* (Chatto and Windus, 1979; Penguin, 1982); French, 1979.

Richard and Anthea are the perfect Sunday supplement couple. ... Sven, Richard's partner in a Scandinavian furniture business, is finally as objective as he boasts he is: Richard has 'flair, something that can't be learnt'. His own mediocre skills are superfluous, he is superfluous. Hugh, a wet vicar, falls in love with Anthea — so inexorably one suspects one sees it even before the playwright. At the same moment he dismisses the possibility she can return his love. Brian was in silent and undeclared love with Anthea before she met Richard. Now he brings a succession of girl-friends for weekends and is employed by Richard and Sven — trapped by kindness. The women — Louise, Hugh's wife, Sven's wife Olive, and Brian's girlfriends — deceive themselves that they could manage without the help of this model couple. Louise is angry if inarticulate as Anthea effortlessly takes over more and more of her parish duties, though fulfilling the prophecy she becomes less and less able to carry them out herself. Olive, without her husband's brutal honesty, sides with Sven after he has stopped siding with himself. The theme is worldly luck, and Alan Ayckbourn implies that the economy of good fortune is zero-sum. Sven offers Richard's and Anthea's daughter a toast on her eighteenth birthday, in the play's last scene, 'There are some lucky ones among us who we refer to as being born with a silver spoon in their mouths. You, Debbie, have been born with a whole canteen of cutlery'. ... The first scenes of its two acts are shell games, tricky but theatrically effective. The play begins on Guy Fawkes' Night, twelve years ago. Richard organizes fireworks on the tennis court, one corner of which we see, as the other adults watch through the fence. Anthea welcomes their new neighbours, who have just moved into the vicarage adjacent to their property. The title comes from Richard's impulsive immolation of the fence around the garden so that Hugh and Louise might share his and Anthea's larger space. The punch-line to the scene is off-stage as well: Hugh and Louise's problem child puts out the bonfire by urinating. The second act opens with all eyes on and in front of the stage focused on the same corner. Sven has challenged Richard to a long-postponed game of tennis. He serves with earnest venom, so out of condition but straining so hard one expects him to stagger just back into our sight and collapse. (In fact his heart attack comes between this scene and the next and last, four years later.) Like so much of Ayckbourn's work, Joking Apart is superbly technical, setting theatrical problems he can and does solve. The tennis court is another variation on lateral construction, in which juxtaposed sets are used to comic effect (How the Other Half Loves, Bedroom Farce). But this is rather more 'vertical' in the manner of Absurd Person Singular; the couples are shown at weekends at intervals of four years.

Arthur Schmidt, *Plays and Players*, Apr. 1979, p. 31

It does go some way towards combining the truth of *Just Between Ourselves* with some of the fun of *Ten Times Table*. Its most significant feature is the time span it covers — twelve years from start to finish. The characters all ages from their late twenties to their early forties, save one who starts in her late twenties and retreats to eighteen. For it's important when reading *Joking Apart* to remember that Melody/Mandy/Mo/Debbie are intended to be played by the same actress. The play was written when the 38-year-old author was confronted by his eighteen-year-old son, who was suddenly adult and growing more so each passing day.

Ayckbourn, 'Preface', *Joking Apart and Other Plays*

Somebody said: 'Why don't you write about a really nice couple? I'm fed up with all these bloody awful marriages.' I said: 'Yes, I really must get this couple together.' And I suddenly realized that, in creating a happy couple — and there are people on the fringes of our lives: they're never in the centre of our lives, they're people we faintly know, which is why they're quite nebulous — they're not the central people, but they're very important to the play. ... I was interested in seeing them from our other characters' point of view. And from their point of view, as Sven says, 'Every bloody thing he touches goes right!' The misunderstanding of the play is that people often think I was writing a play about Richard and Anthea: I was writing a play about Sven, about us, about the inequalities of life. Why the hell should someone be born with less ability than another? Some people seem, in our lives, to have a natural aptitude for everything. ... I wanted to avoid a 'happy marriage'. I wanted to give them a grounding of less than conventionality. There's a suspicion that Anthea wasn't happy in the past, that things haven't always been that incredible: it was the mating of Richard and Anthea — a second-time-around, in fact — that fused into a sort of ideal oneness where everything came right for her. That's the only reason for that and the fact that it gave Hugh, the vicar who destroys himself in love, a glimmer of hope. Sometimes he thinks: 'Well, if my wife dies, or she leaves me, or we get divorced, I could give up the church and I could go off with Anthea; she could leave Richard'. There's a little door with just a chink of light — awful, really.

Ayckbourn, *Conversations*, p. 122, 124

Ayckbourn nowadays appears to achieve comedy by strenuously resisting it. The best passages in *Joking Apart* take place at bedtime, when nothing in particular is happening. As characters exchange desultory gossip the atmosphere gradually thickens with some new, unsuspected poison. But for fans of his earlier manner, there are still dextrous examples of his skill with offstage tennis and croquet games, and simultaneous action such as the poor vicar's love declaration in the midst of Sven's match to the death. It is a superb and chilling piece of work.

Irving Wardle, *The Times*, 3 Feb. 1978, p. 11

Many of the Ayckbourn plays are about insensitivity, and several about an insensitive bonhomie. Few men were ever as well-meaning as Colin in *Absent Friends*, or as cheerful as Dennis in *Just Between Ourselves*; yet the one managed to leave his friends' nerves and marriages in tatters and the other reduced his wife to catatonia. *Joking Apart* is in the same line, but it is less clear-cut and demands of its audiences much subtler powers of discrimination. Richard and Anthea are authentically generous people, and the accusation flung at their disappearing backs by the agonized Finn, that they seek power over their acquaintances, exposes his envy more than their darker motives. Both can be considerate and tactful. She cannot, after all, help it if the vicar falls in love with her, thus accelerating the breakdown of his wife and marriage, nor if an old admirer wastes his youth bringing down weekend guests who look just like her. She *is* loveable. Nor can he be held responsible for the decline of his partner, Sven, from a proud and officious know-all to a self-proclaimed mediocrity, drained of all confidence and off handedly interrupted by the wife who once worshipped him. He *is* able. They cannot be accused of luring their victims on to the rocks with siren-calls: their very existence is enough to provoke passers-by to shipwreck themselves. ... The last scene, with the visiting derelicts giving empty advice to Anthea's contemptuously polite daughter on her coming-of-age, is as good as anything Ayckbourn has written, justification in itself of his continuing attempt to darken his comedy and deepen our laughter.

Benedict Nightingale, 'The Powers That Be',
New Statesman, 16 Mar. 1979, p. 370

See also:
Lloyd Evans, Gareth and Barbara. *Plays in Review, 1956-1980* (London, 1985), p. 232-35.
Morley, Sheridan, *Shooting Stars* (London, 1983), p. 171.

Sisterly Feelings

A play in four scenes, with alternative versions of Scenes 2 and 3.
First production: Stephen Joseph Th., Scarborough, 11 Jan. 1978
(dir. Ayckbourn; with Alison Skilbeck as Abigail, and Robin Herford as Simon).
First London production: National Th. (Olivier), 3 June 1980
(dir. Ayckbourn and Christopher Morahan; with Penelope Wilton as Abigail, Anna Carteret as Dorcas, Michael Gambon as Patrick, Michael Bryant as Len, Stephen Moore as Simon, Simon Callow as Stafford, and Andrew Cruickshank as Ralph).
Published: French, 1981; with *Taking Steps* (Chatto and Windus, 1981); in *Joking Apart and Other Plays* (Penguin, 1982).

Abigail and Dorcas are the sisters with whose feelings we are

51

concerned, and though Abigail is a housewife and Dorcas works in local radio (producer of two half-hour shows a week) they bear more than a passing resemblance to Goneril and Regan. They have a ga-ga dad, and no mother: in fact they are on their way back from her funeral when we first meet them. Above all there is a young man whom they both fancy, though unlike Shakespeare's Edmund he is in no sense a bastard. He is Simon, their brother's girl-friend's brother, a clean-limbed young man and also chivalrous. At the end of Scene One there is some question as to with which of the two he will walk home. In the end the matter is decided by the toss of a coin, and that toss (which incidentally is left to chance in performance) decides the content of the second scene. For the walk home is the prelude to an affair. Scene Two, whatever happens, is a picnic, and the feasters are the same either way, but their relationships obviously differ. The end of this scene provides another moment of choice that determines the nature of Scene Three; Simon may either be having it off with the same flame or with her rival. That Scene Four should be exactly the same, whatever has happened, is of course its own ironic comment. Abigail and Dorcas may pride themselves on their dissimilarities, but nobody else can notice any; to their despised future sister-in-law, for example, they are both 'hopelessly neurotic and out of touch'. The one crucial difference between them is that Abigail is married; and since Mr. Ayckbourn sees his people less in terms of character than in terms of domestic circumstance this is more than enough to justify his peculiar strategy.

That the Abigail play works the better of the two is a tribute to the old-fashioned rules, both social and dramatic. Much depends, of course, on the quality of the cuckold. Here Abigail is in luck: her husband Patrick is an exemplary mixture of cynicism and complaisance. Professing complete tolerance of his wife's activities, he so contrives, with the utmost politeness, to make her life an embarrassment, while Simon, despite the obvious need for discretion, comes close to duffing him up. He is, besides, most incisively characterized as a man besotted with his job, his house and his car, particularly when they involve mechanical extras. By contrast, Stafford, the gentleman whom Dorcas betrays ('Dorcas's thing', her father calls him), is a stereotype of the half-baked far Left intellectual already worked over (to rather better purpose) in Mr. Ayckbourn's *Ten Times Table*. His jealousy takes far less inventive turns than Patrick's. Scene Three offers a choice of Abigail and Simon going camping, or Dorcas officiating at a cross-country race with Simon one of the favourites. Again Abigail offers the better deal: acute situation comedy as opposed to overworked farce. ... I wish Mr. Ayckbourn had allowed his heroines one head-on collision, rather than confining them to polite fencing with undertones.

Robert Cushman, 'Toss of the Coin', *The Observer*, 4 Feb. 1979

The device has the effect of stimulating actors, irritating stage managers, and infuriating box office staff. By way of an apologia, I can only point out that the device is not employed merely out of cussedness. As I say, the plays are about choice. How much do we really control our lives and do we really make decisions or just think we do? In *Sisterly Feelings*, the last scene is always the same, though the emphasis in playing differs. Not that this is saying that I'm a believer in predestination and the inevitability of fate, but rather that I do believe that mostly we finish up with the friends and the partners in life that we deserve. Of course, this variable device is an extremely theatrical one.

Ayckbourn, 'Preface', *Sisterly Feelings and Taking Steps*

There's a whole family in *Sisterly Feelings*. I'm very fascinated by the style of relationships there, because it is totally different from that of a chosen relationship. It is enforced, you're with someone you didn't ask to be with. ... In the case of *Sisterly*, I've implied that Dorcas probably lives away from home for a lot of the time, but that the father, particularly now that he's lost the mother, would need visiting more. All the scenes take place at weekends, so one assumes that that's the time she comes back. And Abigail lives near — none of them actually lives with him — so that's how they're foisted together. In fact, we see them in untypical proximity, because that's the relationship I'm interested in exploring. But I find there is in many relationships — certainly parental ones, also I suspect with brothers and sisters — a sort of love-hate. ...

Unlike a lot of plays which say you always get married to the wrong person, it also says that you always get married to the right person: if you don't like them, it's probably your fault for being the sort of person you are. You've got the person you deserve. I think Abigail has Patrick because she needs Patrick; and Patrick does for her what a big, glorious, bronzed idiot can get nowhere near doing for her.

Ayckbourn, *Conversations*, p. 117, 119, 155

Sisterly Feelings is brilliantly, wickedly funny, but the bleakness underlying so much of Alan's view of life seems in a way to be increasing. The play is about decisions, the moment of choice, whether to change your life or not, and the consequent calamities and happinesses. ... It is a joy to behold such craft, such perception, such absurdity.

Peter Hall, *Diaries* (London, 1983), p. 395, 406

It is all monstrously clever, but it seems rather artifically contrived. Mr. Ayckbourn, having apparently nothing to say, pays excessive attention to his way of saying it. But there are some admirable things in the play, especially the scene in which an apparent moron, played by Selena Cadell [as Brenda], stuns everybody by suddenly bursting into a speech on the economics of setting up a toy shop with a financial mastery of detail which would do credit to any Chancellor of the Exchequer.

Harold Hobson, 'Hobson's Choice', *Drama*, Oct. 1980, p. 42

Priestley in *Dangerous Corner* suggested that a chance remark can change the course of people's lives: Ayckbourn, more cynically, shows people constantly returning to square one. But what makes the play so funny is the contrast between the people who at least exercise choice and those who are totally immutable. ... The one weakness in the design is that Abigail's fling is much more engrossing than Dorcas's: quite simply, there is much more comedy in breaking the marriage vow than cheating on a lover. But this is no reflection on the performances which are splendidly balanced. Anna Carteret's Dorcas alternates excellently between militaristic bossiness and real devotion. but Penelope Wilton's hot-tempered Abigail has the funnier scenes, particularly the night under canvas which ends with a drunken striptease mistaken by the police for a witch's dance.

Michael Billington, *The Guardian*, 4 June 1980

A brilliantly contrived set by Alan Tagg — a grassy hillock in a public park with bushes and a bench — gives masses of space for movement, and Ayckbourn, who co-directs with Christopher Morahan, gets a lot of laughs from his characters' physical exertions. He treats the theatre like an enjoyable toy (indeed he has his own to play with at home in Scarborough) and obviously adores testing his naturalistic ingenuity against the challenges of athletics, bicycling, kite-flying and camping. He requires his characters to be as expressive, and as funny, in facial and bodily gesture as in the delivery of their lines and seems to have invented a non-verbal language as characteristically Ayckbournian as his nonchalant-sounding prose; Stephen Moore, who plays the gormless Simon, is its chief exponent. He is a master too (Ayckbourn that is) of the running gag, the wait-for-it, wait-for-it joke, the old joke in new garb and the old joke in its original garb — indeed of all what might be called the music hall arts. Sometimes he writes beautifully economical lines — like Abigail's description of a witch's coven: 'nudes dancing, dead poultry'.

Peter Jenkins, 'Games of Chance', *Spectator*, 14 June 1980, p. 23

Taking Steps

A farce in two acts.

First production: Stephen Joseph Th., Scarborough, 27 Sept. 1979
(dir. Ayckbourn; with Robin Herford as Mark and Lavinia Bertram as Kitty).

First London production: Lyric Th., 3 Sept. 1980
(dir. Michael Rudman; with Dinsdale Landen as Roland,
Nicola Pagett as Elizabeth, Paul Chapman as Mark, and
Wendy Murray as Kitty).

First American production; York Th. Co., 28 Oct. 1986
(dir. Alex Dmitriev; with Rudolph Willrich as Roland).

Published; French, 1981; with *Sisterly Feelings* (Chatto and Windus, 1981).

It has a recognizable Ayckbourn technical trick, whereby three floors of a rambling Victorian house, worm-ridden and damp, are compressed on to the unelevated stage level. The actors mime running up and down stairs, from the lounge to the master-bedroom to the attic, missing each other by inches or flights; and the director, Michael Rudman, is exceptionally skilful in keeping the different areas defined. Life is in flux. The house has not yet been sold by the desperate builder, Leslie Bainbridge, to the affluent Roland Crabbe, whose marriage to Elizabeth, a dancer, is also in doubt. Elizabeth's brother, Mark, has been trying to marry Kitty for some time; but she will keep running away or falling asleep when he talks to her, and Kitty herself does not know what she wants to do because people keep giving her good advice. It is time for everything to be sorted out, and there is a solicitor on hand, the singularly indecisive Tristram, to help them do so; but the more steps are taken, the more negligible is the progress. In an oblique tribute to Travers,

Ayckbourn includes some Aldwych farce situations — a ghost story as in Thark, *a squiffy-eyed bully and a virgin ditherer who finds himself always compromised, a sweet young thing and a well-intentioned yobbo. ... Dinsdale Landen's Roland is wonderfully funny, bumping down non-existent stairs or gazing at cross-purposes with a tumbler of Scotch.*

John Elsom, 'Me, Myself and I', *Listener*, 11 Sept. 1980, p. 349

I have written very little true farce. Some of my comedies have touched on the farcical but *Taking Steps* is really my first since *How the Other Half Loves*. It was written, like all my plays, for the Theatre in the Round at Scarborough. In this type of theatre, doors, the staple diet of most farces, are really impractical. So I've substituted floors instead. This is, I hope, a play you can enjoy on many levels at once.

Ayckbourn, 'Author's Note', Scarborough programme

It's a play about innocence and proposes the probably naive and certainly unfashionable view that good will triumph (in this case in the shape of the luckless Tristram Watson). It is also about freedom, a subject which preoccupies both the women in the play, Both are trapped — one physically as well as spiritually. Both make bids for freedom. But whereas Kitty is prepared to chance everything to achieve it, Elizabeth would still like to take a small slice of cake with her to eat later.

Ayckbourn, 'Preface', *Sisterly Feelings and Taking Steps*, p. ix

It contains plenty of references to brothels and prostitution — always good for a laugh; half the cast spends half its time in pyjamas, staggering about and falling over; an innocent young man is manouevred into two occupied beds, one after the other; a note is ambiguously worded to give the impression that someone has done himself in. Misunderstandings abound. People are for ever tumbling out of cupboards and getting caught between the sides of a folding bed.

Patricia Craig, 'Upstairs, Downstairs', *Times Literary Supplement*, 19 Sept. 1980, p. 1038

[In the title, Ayckbourn] has covered the whole show in two words which refer at once to the folly of applying strong-arm methods to personal relationships, and to Alan Tagg's set which squashes a three-storey house elevation to stage floor level. ... Much of the comedy consists of hustling separate groups through the house missing each other by split seconds. This is carried out with the wizardry we lazily take for granted from this playwright. To see the surveying party tramping the corridors while the wife lurks to make a dash at the front door; or to observe Watson left alone in a darkened room while a brisk, fully-lit debate takes place a few inches away from him, is to see Ayckbourn's gift for acrobatic comedy stretched to the full. ... For once, Ayckbourn is not relying for his laughs on unsupported human nature. Details like the appearance of the landlord in black motorbike kit, the house's history (a haunted brothel), and numerous extravagant bits of plotting (a misattributed suicide note, a mistaken identity brawl), add up to an impression of strained departure from plausible behaviour.

Irving Wardle, *The Times*, 3 Sept. 1980, p. 11

Suburban Strains

A musical, with music by Paul Todd.
First production: Stephen Joseph Th., Scarborough, 18 Jan. 1980
    (dir. Ayckbourn; with Lavinia Bertram as Caroline and Robin Herford as Matthew).
First London production: Round House, 5 Feb. 1981 (the Scarborough production).
Published: French, 1982.

The central figure is Caroline, a schoolteacher who flees from marriage with an actor, who messes up both her flat and her life, to an affair with a doctor who tries tyrannically to tidy them up. The treatment is generally chronological, but with leaps; moments from the first relationship are frequently recalled, to be juxtaposed with the second. On the outskirts are grimly cheerful dinner-parties and pep-talks from Caroline's appallingly optimistic newsagent dad, backed — in the happiest musical stroke of the evening — by a trio of OAP customers. ... Two concentric revolves have been installed, the actors generally standing in the inner circle while necessary furnishings travel to them on the outer.

Robert Cushman, 'Distant Laughter', *The Observer*, 27 Jan. 1980

It's really a musical play, more *Teeth'n'Smiles* than *Oklahoma*! I've found that Paul Todd's music actually helps me as a playwright; it's given me that necessary kick beyond naturalism. You have an equivalent of the soliloquy — no need for a boring old drunk scene to make characters say what they feel. If you suddenly bring in a shaft of music from somewhere, they can actually play the subtext. Generally the English prefer to hint round the truth, which is fun and leads to a lot of comedy, but for me it's been very interesting to find this other dimension. ... Caroline, the central character, has been hanging around me a long time. I'm very fond of her: lovely, silly, quirky girl. It's the first time I've every created a star part, who carries the play and makes us see the events — her relationships — through her eyes. She's 32 and a teacher, more or less untroubled by a personal life, and then along comes this actor who's young and fun and a total opposite. When the relationship breaks up, she says 'I've got the balance all wrong, I was too dominating, now I'll be feminine'. But her next man is a big mistake. There's a lot of me in her. Trying to give what you hope will be the right reaction, which quite often it isn't.

Ayckbourn, interviewed by Anthony Masters,
'The Essentially Ambiguous Response', *The Times*, 4 Feb. 1981, p. 8

A new Ayckbourn theme — glimpsed in *Taking Steps* — is beginning to appear: the need to resist other people's expectations.

Robert Cushman, *The Observer*, 8 Feb. 1981

The play's first half, chronicling the collapse of pernickety Caroline's marriage to slovenly Kevin, covers ground he hasn't so much trodden as worn down to the subterranean limestone. ... The second half is better, thanks to a climactic supper and to two nice additions to Ayckbourn's human bestiary: a plump capon named Howard, whose obsession is food, and a superbly complacent doctor, whose obsession is tidiness and whose function is to reconcile Caroline to mess and Kevin. All along Caroline has been a natural victim, like the put-upon Annie in *The Norman Conquests*. Friends and relations have always patronized, blamed or reviled her, or simply used her adversity as an excuse to talk about themselves. Now she finds her voice, carriage, breasts, feet, manners and conduct endlessly subjected to her new lover's built-in X-ray machine; and for a moment it looks as if she, like Vera before her, may actually be destroyed by the cumulative pressure and the play end where Ayckbourn's work so often has of late, in the dumps. She isn't, and it doesn't.

Benedict Nightingale, 'Gravamen', *New Statesman*, 13 Feb. 1981, p. 22

Suburban Strains is not particularly about the suburbs, but about a marriage and specifically about the view from the woman's side of the gulf. Unlike most plays in that sour modern genre it gives you an inkling of how the protagonists might once have fancied, liked and loved one another. Consequently, despite an artificially sweetened ending, its ironic pessimism is more persuasive than the ranting of most attacks on the institutionalized relationship. ... Todd's fifteen or so songs make a lightweight evening into a rather long one and tend to embellish it rather than move it on, except on one or two occasions, such as the sharply recognizable agony of 'What Does She Expect of Me?'

Paul Allen, 'Good-Time', *New Statesman*, 25 Jan. 1980, p. 142

The evening might have been designed as an anthology of all the tired and emotional clichés that have made the British musical a byword for enervation and flaccidity. ... Todd's tunes are limper still, a sort of Sondheim-and-*Salad Days* with the zip missing.

Hilary Spurling, 'Side by Side in Scarborough',
Times Literary Supplement, 13 Feb. 1981

Mr. Ayckbourn and Mr. Todd seem to have no greater intention than to tell a small story pleasantly. That is what they achieve.

Ned Chaillet, *The Times*, 6 Feb. 1981, p. 11

Season's Greetings

A comedy in two acts.
First production: Stephen Joseph Th., Scarborough, 25 Sept. 1980
  (dir. Ayckbourn; with Robin Herford as Harvey and Lavinia Bertram
  as Pattie).
First London production: Round House, 14 Oct. 1980 (transfer of
  Scarborough production).
Revival: Greenwich Th., 28 Jan. 1982 (dir. Ayckbourn; with Diane Bull
  as Pattie, Barbara Ferris as Belinda, Bridget Turner as Phyllis, and
  Nigel Havers as Clive); transferred to Apollo Th., 29 Mar. 1982
  (same cast except Christopher Strauli as Clive).
First American production: Berkeley Rep. Th., California, Spring 1984
  (dir. Douglas Johnson).
First New York production: Joyce Th., 6 July 1985 (dir. Pat Brown)
  (transferred from Alley Th., Houston).
Television production: BBC-2, 24 Dec. 1986 (dir. Michael Simpson;
  with Bridget Turner as Phyllis, Anna Massey as Rachel,
  Nicky Henson as Neville, and Geoffrey Palmer as Bernard).
Published: French, 1982.

[The Christmas] goings-on at Neville and Belinda's are a happy compendium of expected marital misfortunes. Neville takes refuge in his shed with his machines, while Belinda fumes about his uselessness around the house. Pattie and Eddie have a similar difficulty compounded by Eddie's total incapacity as a businessman and the imminence of yet another child. Phyllis and Bernard are childless; she drinks and he insists on staging his annual puppet show over the objections of all the adults in sight and to the total boredom of the children he believes he understands. The older folk watch television when Uncle Harvey is not raving on about guns and knives. And the unmarried sister (38, and worried that she may be behaving like an adolescent) brings into all of this a writer who has to cope with illiterate advice from all sides, over-intense personal interest from Belinda and the sort of reaction you might expect from Neville, a man who says with some pride: 'Can't tell you the last time I read a book'.

John Russell Taylor, The Times, 15 Oct. 1980, p. 10

What Rachel wants from [Clive] is a friendship. And it's a sad thing, really, because it seems that you can't have that sort of friendship with a man like Clive. Her sister, who's just bored over Christmas, can have a deeper relationship with him in two seconds underneath the Christmas tree, which she does. In the end, Rachel sort of gets him back, but we all know it's not going to be for long. The next time Clive meets somebody in a theatre queue or somewhere, he'll be off again. ... It's based on my experiences at Christmas. My younger son used to have a puppet show, and I used to come home two days before Christmas, write the script, and get it on. But it was desperately serious and there was no fun to be had anywhere. There was a full technical rehearsal, with a lot of screaming and tears, and: 'Get that dog on the stage!' and: 'That scene change has got to get some time off it!' It was only done for Grandad and Granny, but the work that went into it was wonderful. And puppeteers are very funny: they're quite often hysterical, possessive people who fight a lot.

Ayckbourn, Conversations, p. 170-1

Season's Greetings takes off from *Absurd Person Singular* by being about Christmas and from *Sisterly Feelings* by being about sisters. Again they fight over a man.

Robert Cushman, The Observer, 19 Oct. 1980

Ayckbourn has written very successful plays about nice middle-class people (*Relatively Speaking*, *Bedroom Farce*) and fairly successful plays about nasty middle-class people (*Just Between Ourselves*, *Joking Apart*). ... The people are really the same, it is a question of how deeply they are probed, how sorely they are tried. *Season's Greetings* looks as if it is going to be only fairly successful as the family group for Christmas includes, for instance, a drunken wife, a self-proclaimed failure, who devotes the year to preparing a puppet show which leaves its audience stupefied with boredom, and another, unproclaimed, who is not going to get the job he hopes for from his host. But no, the immensely efficient cast are sent scurrying about a set that manages to include five acting areas, the hell of Yuletide is combined (unconvincingly) with the stranger-enters-and-disrupts-a-family plot and depth is rarely attempted.

Mark Amory, 'Glorious Summer', *The Spectator*, 6 Feb. 1982, p. 28

While writers like Catherine Hayes have great respect for their characters and, thus, their audience, Ayckbourn at his best has little, and at his worst, as here, none at all. The situation is what concerns him. His nine more-or-less excellent players (directed by himself) people the stage as sketchy character-types in pursuit of combustion at the predictable family gathering; there is one nice comic flare in the middle and a hollow bang at the end. At various points it seems as if the author might be heading to an examination of how spinster sister Rachel puts off men; of whether there is some solidity in the dreary marriage of her sexy sister Belinda; of how the perpetually pregnant Pattie can put up with the violent brutishness of the ne'er-do-well Eddie. Between them they add up to Ayckbourn's general, and reiterated, point about women coping better than men, and doing it by being realistically dissatisfied while their spouses scuttle off into obsessiveness or aloofness.

Victoria Radin, *The Observer*, 7 Feb. 1982

The play itself comes close to being Ayckbourn's best: it is the usual family reunion gone wrong, but this time situated at such a perfect mid-point between farce and tragedy that even the failed doctor who seems to have wandered in from *Uncle Vanya* manages to make himself at home.

Sheridan Morley, 'Tour de Force', *Punch*, 10 Feb. 1982, p. 241

The alcoholic wife of a doctor urges [the novelist] to tell her 'all about English literature' — adding 'It is now or never'. But for all of them that Now has long since passed. The best character, at once sweet and sad, is the doctor (a lovely performance from Ronald Herdman) — so hopeless at his job that he has only to pronounce, 'I am afraid this man is dead' for the 'corpse' to emit a groan. ... This Chekhovian work, now glinting with wintry sunlight and now shrouded in a mist of failure and futility, proves highly effective.

Francis King, 'Roman Scandal',
Sunday Telegraph, 19 Oct. 1980, p. 16

Way Upstream

A play in two acts.

First production: Stephen Joseph Th., Scarborough, 2 Oct. 1981
(dir. Ayckbourn; with Robin Herford as Alistair and Lavinia Bertram as Emma).

First American production: Alley Th., Houston, 24 Feb. 1982 (with Scarborough cast).

First London production: National Th., 5 Oct. 1982 (dir. Ayckbourn; with Jim Norton as Alistair, Julie Legrand as Emma, Susan Fleetwood as June, and James Laurenson as Vince).

Television production: 1 Jan. 1988 (adapted and dir. Terry Johnson).

Published: French, 1983.

The boat is the setting for a holiday cruise up the River Orb for two couples, one bossy and assertive, the other sensitive and put-upon. They're partners in a firm that makes fancy goods, and while the bosses are away, their workers take over the factory. Meeting his secretary for daily up-dating, Keith is for taking them on; his wife June just resents the intrusion. But then the play makes another new departure for Ayckbourn, from cosily familiar naturalism into an almost mystical world of fantasy. Normally all his characters are pathetically flawed. Here for the first time we meet real, hard evil. Drifting bully Vince and his titled playgirl friend Fleur move in and take over the boat. Nice, reasonable, and ineffectual, like you and me, Alistair and Emma are the only credible characters in the play. Faced with unreason — aggressive greed on the one hand and violent anarchy on the other — they are forced to assert themselves, and finally emerge alone into the sunlit haven beyond Armageddon Bridge, where they strip off to jump hand-in-hand into the water — the tasteful nudity being another first for Ayckbourn. ...

If it's visually a commercial for the Inland Waterways Association, philosophically it's a plug for the soggy centrism of the Social Democratic Party.

Robin Thornber, *The Guardian*, 5 Oct. 1981

I set this play in a boat because a vast proportion of Britons are stupid enough to believe they come from a seafaring race who go out on the Broads and ram each other.

Ayckbourn, interviewed by Bryan Appleyard,
'Still Hoping for Heroes', *The Times*, 18 Aug. 1982, p. 7

This play was originally produced ... using real water, rain and a moving boat. However, as will become apparent, these are not essential. The play can be produced equally satisfactorily using simulated or imagined water and even a boat with little or no movement.

'Author's Note', *Way Upstream* (French, 1983)

The dreadful truth dawns that this is not any hired cabin cruiser. It is the Ship of Life, and the trip is an allegorical progress from which the timid characters emerge having learned how to say 'yes' to life. The play presents the suicidal spectacle of a playwright driving past the limit of his own talent and coming to a sticky end.

Irving Wardle, 'Ayckbourn's Watery Grave',
The Times, 5 Oct. 1982, p. 8

It is more of a technical curiosity than a stage play. When it's funny, it can be like the best of Ayckbourn. When it goes serious, it seems inadvertently to suggest that violence is a good thing, an excellent way of curing a man of his meekness and his sexual hang-ups.

James Fenton, 'Why All that Glitters Is Not Gold',
Sunday Times, 10 Oct. 1982, p. 43

Upstream, it transpires, takes us out of *Three Men in a Boat* country into somewhere more like *Straw Dogs Afloat*. ... Whether interpreted politically (the need for the moderate centre to assert itself against extremism), metaphysically (the inevitability of confronting evil on its own terms), or psychologically (a voyage back through the jungle of our base instincts to the lost innocence of the womb), *Way Upstream* leaves an uneasy sense of events, and characters, manipulated to fit a pattern. Elsewhere in Ayckbourn's *oeuvre*, intimations of pain, humiliation and eventual precarious harmony have sprouted more naturally from the comic groundsoil. Here, his material seems to be loaded with more significance that it can finally bear.

Philip Kemp, 'English Manners', *Sight and Sound*,
Winter 1987, p. 288 [of the television version]

Keith himself says that his wife's function in life is 'decoration'; for a long time Fleetwood's strident, glamourized, bikini-clad figure [as June], one of those ball-breaking sexpots similar to the Beverley of *Abigail's Party* (Ayckbourn often being not unlike a scripted Mike Leigh), is a very elaborate work of characterization which deflects, as no one else on stage, our attention from the boat. Eventually, however, Ayckbourn brings on Vince. ... The drama, which the programme tells us is to terminate at Armageddon Bridge, begins. It is sadistic and nasty. It is also, between the lines, a hymn to the solid virtues of the middle-class couple (one of the worst things about Vince and Fleur is that they are promiscuous). It is also entirely implausible. It ends with all the baddies routed and Emma and Keith alone, naked to one another for the first time (spiritually, anyway), poised for a dive into a Jungian sea of sex. The ship equals Life, of course; and its wayward trajectory, life's impulse to disintegration. That's a venerable metaphor, and I don't chide Ayckbourn for that. What is bad is that he hasn't given us enough information on his people to make their harrowing important. Nor can I believe that people are totally divided between the meek and the megalomaniac.

Victoria Radin, 'Chinks in the Panto',
The Observer, 10 Oct. 1982, p. 32

The final moments of *Way Upstream* constitute a sort of corny Shavian apotheosis not unlike that of *Heartbreak House*.

Michael Coveney, *Financial Times*, 6 Oct. 1982

Ayckbourn has said he wanted to write about evil, and his play suggests he's also trying to give it a socio-political dimension. Alistair and Emma, it seems, are the decent but unassertive moderates, beset by the threat of fascism (Vince), the spoiled rich (Fleur), capitalism (Keith), labour (a briefly glimpsed striker), and whatever generality the shiftless June represents. But they survive, to find new togetherness and strength on the other side of Armageddon Bridge (!), where they prepare for a crusading return to nasty reality, after the manner of the socialists of Priestley's *They Came to a City*: 'We reasonable people will have to go back and reason with them'. Now, Ayckbourn's long-held aim has been to deepen his work and our laughter. Does he succeed in this, or is his river-saga simply an over-important *Swallows and Amazons*, an instance of comic dramatist getting out of his depth, even sinking into a watery grave? Well, I don't think the play altogether works, either on a personal or a supra-personal level. ... It's surely inspiring to find our leading comic dramatist insisting on setting improbable new challenges for himself.

> Benedict Nightingale, 'All in the Same Boat',
> *New Statesman*, 8 Oct. 1982, p.27-8

As in Priestley's *Bees on the Boatdeck*, the boat represents England, civilization, decency or what-you-will. ... The transition from the kind of rueful comedy for which Ayckbourn is rightly famous to the horror of one of the wives suffering sexual degradation, the other being forced to walk the plank, and one of the husbands slugging it out with the male intruder, is nothing short of masterly.

> Francis King. 'The Sins of the Forefathers',
> *Sunday Telegraph*, 10 Oct. 1982, p. 18

The journey of the nice people up the river named after the world through to the far side of Armageddon has been described in my hearing as a party political broadcast for the Social Democrats. ... I prefer to believe it is something related to that but at once both more simple and more deeply significant, the statement of a profound myth which the English cherish above all that the nice guys eventually win through. ... I don't myself think the play finally supports this myth, not in the sense of giving it the force of realism, whether intended or not. The final 'frozen frame' of the nice couple poised naked over the water while already bathed in a warm light told me that the whole story was a hymn to wishful thinking.

> Paul Allen, 'North', *Drama*, Spring 1982, p. 46

Making Tracks

A musical: music by Paul Todd.
First production: Stephen Joseph Th., Scarborough, 16 Dec. 1981
(dir. Ayckbourn).

First London production: Greenwich Th., 14 Mar. 1983
  (dir. Ayckbourn).
Unpublished.

---

*Set in a recording studio, it poses the problem faced by the
desperate impresario Stan, whose future depends on discovering
a star and making a hit record — in a hurry. A bullying tycoon
to whom he owes money demands it back with menaces, and
locks him and his musicians in the studio with a waif-like girl
Stan has discovered when over-excited. She has only to open her
mouth to sound like a singing road-accident. With the help of the
tycoon's mistress, Lace, Stan's former partner in writing songs,
he hopes to save his bacon. But Lace has quarrelled with him,
and won't cooperate. That is the situation, and it stays static
until the happy end, guessable from half-way point if you know
anything about musical comedy. It is enlivened, however, by
some moderately lively Ayckbourn dialogue. ... The show is
most resourceful in its witty use of sound-recording jargon. Talk
of mixing, replay, receiving and fading applies neatly to any off-
on love affair.*

John Barber, Daily Telegraph, 15 Mar. 1983

It has the unusual Ayckbourn characteristics of being both derivative and
sentimental. It also includes songs from Paul Todd which instead of
progressing the action, as in the best musicals, halt it stone dead. ...
Presumably Ayckbourn was attracted to the mechanical possibilities of a
studio: the sound-proof glass, the array of props that could go
disastrously wrong, the pretensions of the pop music business. ... There
is a woeful lack of character development and psychological insight
from our leading interpreter of modern *mores*.

Antony Thorncroft, Financial Times, 15 Mar. 1983

The one thing Ayckbourn fails to convey is any sense of a race against
time. The company may be flat out doing last-minute rewrites, but at the
cue for a song they are up on their feet belting out pastiche Caribbean
and Doris Day favourites. ... Suspense apart, it is hard to believe in any
of these people: the drummer who has to get back to a birthday tea (for
his dead father!), the hard-bitten sound-engineer who mysteriously falls
for the hopeless Sandy, or the obligatory comic character Ayckbourn

introduces in the second half.

> Irving Wardle, 'Brake on Action', *The Times*, 15 Mar. 1983, p. 15

At its best, the show is an ingenious concoction of lowbrow comedy, good timing, bad jokes, impressive stagecraft and seamless plotting. At its worst it is a tedious blend of superficial wit and vapid sentimentality, dragged further down by performances which are exaggerated to the point of ridicule.

> Rosalind Carne, *The Guardian*, 15 Mar. 1983

Intimate Exchanges

A play in four scenes, with sixteen variants.

First production: Stephen Joseph Th., Scarborough, 3 June 1982 (dir. Ayckbourn; with Robin Herford playing all male parts and Lavinia Bertram playing all female parts); the variants were added steadily until all sixteen were played in two weeks in Spring 1983.

First London production: Greenwich Th., 11 June 1984 (Scarborough production: eight variants for one week each), transferred to Ambassador's Th., 10 Aug. 1984.

Published: French (two vols.), 1986.

At the very start of Intimate Exchanges, *a woman is faced with a small, fairly trivial decision. Should she resist having that first cigarette of the day before 6.00 p.m.? On some nights, her will power is strong enough; on others it isn't. The two quite separate chains of events that result from her choice lead, by the end of Scene One, to another character making two further decisions, this time of a slightly more important nature. Just before the interval two more choices, more crucial still, are to be made. Finally, preceding the fourth and final scene, another two major courses of action remain to be chosen by the characters. What you will see tonight then, is a single strand of a much larger web of interconnecting alternative scenes. Each evening is intended to be complete in itself although it will, of course, be only ever one version of what might have happened if. I hope curiosity will bring you back to see some of the other 'ifs'.*

> Ayckbourn, programme note

[The above means that there are two first scenes, four second scenes, eight third scenes and sixteen fourth scenes. In all variants, the time-gap between the first two scenes is five days, between the second and third five weeks, and between the third and fourth five years. Further, the first two scenes always take place in the garden of the home of a prep. school headmaster, the third scene in 'any one of several places', and the fourth always in a churchyard — though the occasions include a christening, a wedding, a funeral, a midnight mass and a harvest festival. To complicate his task still further, Ayckbourn has written for one male and one female actor, who may play up to three or four different parts in any one variant.]

The theme is marital discontent, focusing this time on the staff and officials of a ... school. Toby, the headmaster, is a drunk; Celia, his wife, is on the point of bolting back to mother; Miles, the Chairman of the Governors, fancies Celia; and his wife Rowena is having an affair with the PE teacher. ... The first night trip led over some well-landscaped comic territory.

> Irving Wardle, 'Another Ayckbourn, Another Hit',
> *The Times*, 7 June 1982, p. 10

Given that there may well be eight different ways of writing *Intimate Exchanges*, most playwrights would I think have discarded seven of them and given us a final draft pulling together the best of the rewrites. Mr. Ayckbourn, not a man to waste much, is throwing all eight at his audiences and letting them decide which ones they like best.

> Sheridan Morley, 'Twin Sets', *Punch*, 20 June 1984, p. 54

Ayckbourn suburbia unrolls before us: put-upon wives, alcoholics, the cheerfully ineffectual, the fantasists, the disapproved of and envied — the middle class, in short, teetering on the brink of corporate incomprehension as it flounders through cross-purposes, dreams and disappointments. ... On the credit side ... is the new complexity of Ayckbourn's men. Toby is not the crassly unfeeling bully found in *Just Between Ourselves* or *Absent Friends*. He reads *The Guardian* and his extensive hates include the police as well as pornography, 'filthy floodlit cricket', and the price of whisky.

> Martin Hoyle, *Financial Times*, 12 June 1984

The whole thing is arrogant, demented and mesmerizing. Ayckbourn assumes, and it seems rightly, that people will go more than once to watch different things happen to the same people in much the same settings. Of course, sitcom audiences do this all the time; but here the point of each version is that it actually cancels all the others. ... The dialogue has a flinty accuracy, and a spell-binding alertness to the moods of dim and difficult people who are long on suffering and short on patience. Ayckbourn deploys all his dexterity to tell us that all plays are unreal; but also that they can feel every bit as real as life. These plays are situation tragedies: their collective title refers to what promises to be a series of dismal disloyalties, mostly marital, with all their pain and grotesque humiliations. They chronicle the enchanting hamfistedness of the English in love.

> John Peter, 'Puffing Graciously down the Last Lap',
> *Sunday Times*, 24 June 1984, p. 39

'The extraordinary thing is that he's been able to people the stage with so many characters', Robin [Herford] said. One of the local councillors confessed he thought there were more in the cast. Robin thought it was intended consciously to develop the convention. On one occasion he exits and darts back across the stage as a minor character, apparently for no reason. He suspects Ayckbourn put that in as a deliberate tease. For Lavinia [Bertram] some of the quick changes can be a strain — she is sometimes calling dialogue from offstage in one character while changing into the costume and persona of another. 'What Alan wants is a bit of a nod and a wink to the audience', she says. 'It's worked very well with people who have got to know the characters'. ... Both the actors and, apparently, audiences had found the characters filled out as they saw more versions. Robin says, 'It's a weird sensation. Normally when you get a script, that's all you're going to know about that character. With this you keep learning more as you do more versions, and you find yourself thinking, ah, *that's* what he meant.' ... He thinks Ayckbourn had two purposes in writing it. 'A, there's the way the tiniest decision can change the whole pattern of your life. B, it's also saying that within relationships there are patterns for further relationships, so there is a resonance to it.' ... Lavinia: 'In one of the plays Rowena (Miles's wife) sums it up when she says, "Much as you search for fresh pastures very little is liable to happen unless you first change yourself".'

> Robin Thornber, 'Ayckbourn's Monster in the Wings',
> *The Guardian*, 29 Oct. 1982, p. 11

A Trip to Scarborough

'Variations on an original play by Sheridan' [also *A Trip to Scar-borough*, which in fact was based on Vanbrugh's *The Relapse*].

First production: Stephen Joseph Th., Scarborough, 8 Dec. 1982
   (dir. Ayckbourn).
Unpublished.

Ayckbourn's A Trip to Scarborough *takes Sheridan's as a starting point but sets most of it in the entrance-hall of a posh hotel in twentieth-century Scarborough. Ayckbourn is an experienced professional in modern farce, so it is not surprising to see that he's blown Sheridan's unification of Vanbrugh's double-plot sky high, and turned it into three, not two, disconnected plots set in three distinct historical periods — 1800, 1940 and 1980 — only associated by the nominal continuity provided by the names of the characters (as they change periods their names modify, so that Sir Tunbelly Clumsy becomes Sir George Tunberry and Wing Commander Tunbry by turn, and the other characters follow suit).*

Hugh Haughton, 'Alteration and Circulation',
Times Literary Supplement, 7 Jan. 1983

What you look for in vain is any purposeful connection — apart from the pursuit of money — between the different plots. Sheridan's characters keep cropping up with slightly altered names; and, just as Hoyden will do anything to escape Sir Tunbelly, so will Holly to get free from Sir George Tunberry. But, if you seize on that as a key to the remaining characters, it does not fit. Tom might perhaps be reborn as a hell-raising flight-lieutenant, but not as a sales rep making nudging inquiries about Scarborough's red light district. Most mysterious of all is that final transformation of Loveless and the light-fingered major into a speechlessly bashful Mr. Love checking in for his honeymoon. ... The doubling and time-shifts are great fun.

Irving Wardle, *The Times*, 13 Dec. 1982, p. 10

It Could Be Any One of Us

A play.
First production: Stephen Joseph Th., Scarborough, 5 Oct. 1983
   (dir. Ayckbourn).

The play is set in the drawing room of what is clearly a large and lonely mock Tudor mansion (another delicious design from Edward Lipscomb) inhabited by a wealthy eccentric family with artistic pretensions. The eldest brother, Mortimer, a failed composer, controls the cash. Tightly. He blames his failure on the family — brother Brinton, a failed artist; sister Jocelyn, a failed novelist; Herman Norris, an insurance assessor who doesn't seem to have been too successful either; and her sullen daughter, Amy, who does nothing but eat. To vent his spleen he threatens to dispossess them all by leaving the property to a near stranger, a former pupil he invites for the weekend, thus providing them all with motive and opportunity.

Robin Thornber, *The Guardian*, 7 Oct. 1983

I have long been attracted by the thought of writing a play that fits that currently rather unfashionable description, a comedy thriller. Here it is at last. It has, I hope, one or two differences. For instance, the villain tends to vary from night to night. So do come and see it — and, by all means, tell your friends who did it — it's unlikely to be the same when they come.

Ayckbourn, Stephen Joseph Th. publicity leaflet

The big scene is delightful, with the terrified Miss Bertram [Lavinia Bertram as the visiting ex-pupil] picking out ever more excruciating nursery ditties on the piano in a howling storm, but it only emphasizes the play's weakness in wedding this particular brand of theatrical algebra to such a spectacle of human vulnerability. ... Ayckbourn's ingenuity, I fear, has created a multiple thriller that works only as a logical machine — and not always too logically at that.

Anthony Masters, *The Times*, 10 Oct. 1983, p. 13

A Chorus of Disapproval

A comedy in two acts.
First production: Stephen Joseph Th., Scarborough, 2 May 1984 (dir. Ayckbourn).
First London production: Olivier Th., 1 Aug. 1985 (dir. Ayckbourn; with Michael Gambon as Dafydd, Bob Peck as Guy Jones,

Imelda Staunton as Hannah, and Gemma Craven as Fay); transferred to Lyric Th., 4 June 1986 (many cast changes including Colin Blakely as Dafydd).

First American production: Contemporary Th., Seattle, 14 July 1988 (dir. Jeff Steitzer).

Film: script by Ayckbourn and Michael Winner (dir. Michael Winner; with Anthony Hopkins as Dafydd, and Jeremy Irons as Guy Jones), for release in 1989.

Published: French, 1985; Faber, 1986.

A brilliantly imaginative and funny comedy of life, sex and sadness in a small town amateur operatic society during rehearsals for The Beggar's Opera. *... Guy Jones, the Candide of Alternative Forward Costing, rises through the cast of Gay's opera from Crook-Fingered Jack to the role of Macheath himself as others drop out or make way for him in the belief that he possesses important industrial knowledge about the plans of his multinational employer in the town. Being Guy, he possesses no such thing. Also being Guy, he is too obtuse to see that this information is expected of him in return for favours received and he is as shocked as everyone else when, far from expanding, the firm closes down and he gets the sack. By then,* The Beggar's Opera *has enjoyed a tearful triumph in the Joshua Pike Memorial Centre Complex and nobody in the cast is speaking to him.*

Michael Ratcliffe, 'Beggaring Neighbours',
The Observer, 4 Aug. 1985, p. 19

Even the best scene, in which the deceived Dafydd confides his wife's frigidity, ends in a shameless borrowing from *Confusions* (someone has switched on the Tannoy). No amount of shrewd observation of amateur dramatic ruthlessness, hysteria and tantrums can disguise all the recycling. The fur-coated *prima donna* last wore her crinoline in *Ten Times Table*. The old seam, at least, appears to be finally worked out.

Anthony Masters, *The Times*, 4 May 1984, p. 13

The complexity of the characters hearteningly illustrates Ayckbourn's constantly ripening gifts. Guy may struggle to preserve his integrity (with the Ayckbourn irony, he ends up despised, vilified and mistrusted) but, no mere goody, he greedily grabs sexual gratification when available, no matter how unsuitable. Similarly, the downtrodden wife (a familiar Ayckbourn figure) is here a worm capable of turning and snatching ruthlessly at happiness, even if it means hurting others. And the archetypal Ayckbourn husband — crass, apparently unloving — is not simply the manipulating bully of *Absent Friends* or the blandly obtuse ignoramus of *Just Between Ourselves*; he is infuriatingly self-absorbed but vulnerable, vaguely aware of his own weaknesses and perhaps capable of a decency Guy somehow misses. Michael Gambon is shambling and bear-like where Scarborough's Russell Dixon was stockily flabby. The latter was more convincing as a not too successful small-town solicitor dabbling in sharp practice; but Gambon excels at the amateur theatrical, more florid (as always happens) than the professional.

Martin Hoyle, *Plays and Players*, Oct. 1985, p. 30-1

These people are, without doubt, the most unpleasant bunch to be gathered on stage since *The Little Foxes*, with one possible exception, the Welsh director. ... Listening to these creatures' diversified accents, it began to dawn on me that perhaps Mr. Ayckbourn is exhibiting for us a cross-section of today's society, that 'Lower Middle Class' which, according to John Osborne, are 'taking over', and which are the unlovely denizens of Mrs. Thatcher's England. Viewed in this light, *A Chorus of Disapproval* becomes much more than the 'good laugh' which most of the audience seemed to be enjoying on the night I saw it. Would they find it so funny if they looked beneath the comical surface and realized exactly who and what they were laughing at?

Sandy Wilson, *Plays International*, July 1986, p. 28-9

Ayckbourn's real subject is suburban man's casual, petty beastliness to suburban man, and the indignation and bewilderment of small minds with large ambitions. He belongs to the comic tradition of Jonson and Molière, but with the important difference that he's entirely free of preachifying, and even his most vitriolic observations are tinged with the wry and spontaneous sympathy of a fellow creature. This is moral comedy in the best sense: Ayckbourn is not afraid to like his creations.

John Peter, 'The Art of Survival', *Sunday Times*, 4 Aug. 1985, p. 43

See also:
Michael Billington, 'Stage to Screen, via Scarborough', *New York Times*, 5 June 1988, H29, H42 [the film].

Woman in Mind

Subtitled 'December Bee'; a play in two acts.
First production: Stephen Joseph Th., Scarborough, 30 May 1985
    (dir. Ayckbourn; with Ursula Jones as Susan).
First London production: Vaudeville Th., 3 Sept. 1986 (dir. Ayckbourn;
    with Julia McKenzie as Susan, Martin Jarvis as Gerald, and
    Peter Blythe as Bill).
First New York production: Manhattan Th. Club, 17 Feb. 1988
    (dir. Lynne Meadow; with Stockard Channing as Susan, and
    Simon Jones as Bill).
Published: French, 1986; Faber, 1986.

A bilious, raw, strange and surreal account of a married woman's dissatisfactions and hallucinated family counterparts after she has knocked herself out on the garden rake. The play opens and closes with fast re-wound gibberish, as if Susan's nightmare is a symptom of concussed sensibility. Attended by a doctor who has admired her secretly from afar, she is greeted by a white-clad trio of ideal husband, young brother and brilliant daughter with tennis court chatter and offers of champagne. They would all be lost without her. ... Susan is married to a boring vicar, Gerald, whom Martin Jarvis, thickening gloriously into comic middle age, presents as a lumpen, patronizing cleric whose offertory gestures have been recycled for domestic tyranny, whose light and skidding Sunday morning pleasantries have hardened into whip-lash phrases of conciliation and contempt. They are expecting their son Rick for lunch, a boy who has joined a set in Hemel Hempstead and communicates with his father only through the odd letter. He does not speak to his mother. Gerald's sister Muriel (the goggle-eyed, angular Josephine Tewson) is also on hand, preparing hideous omelettes and undrinkable coffee while hoping that her deceased bedridden husband will somehow get in touch. ... When Rick breaks his silence and threatens to decamp to Thailand with a nurse he has already married, Susan consigns him to the fantasy. By now, her Furies, or voices, or whatever, have assumed a more menacing shape and a ghostly row culminates in an act of sexual possession on the lawn. While a storm rages, the doctor is thrown

in the lake, Gerald's manuscript burnt, and Muriel's 'Harry' is
reported back from the dead. With an outrageous switch of mood
and tempo, a wedding party becomes a day at the races and the
two worlds merge in a vivid social and ecclesiastical tableau.

Michael Coveney, *Financial Times*, 4 Sept. 1986

I wanted to write a first-person narrative, a play seen, like a film,
through the lens of a hand-held camera. A play that would do the very
thing one is careful to avoid as a dramatist. That is, break the rules,
undermine normal logic, slowly rob the situation of reality. ... I thought
it would be fun to write about a woman who invented a dream family
because her own was so disappointing and so boring. And I wanted to
introduce the sort of imaginary people we'd all like to know, however
much we may deny it. Unashamedly romantic, very high gloss, way over
the top, as if from some super soap opera, full of laughter and flashing
teeth. ... We see what Susan sees yet doesn't see. We glimpse the
characters, as it were, over her shoulder. By the end, the audience should
realize it's thrown in its lot with someone who isn't altogether to be
trusted, either in her opinions or her perceptions.

Ayckbourn, quoted by Benedict Nightingale,
'A Woman of Two Minds, Both in Turmoil',
New York Times, 14 Feb. 1988, H5

Ayckbourn's ingenuity and audacity run ahead of his sensibility. He is
a very prosaic playwright, which is why even his best work seems
strangely muffled. I wanted Susan's dream to be more than a tying
together of motifs, just as I wanted Guy in *A Chorus of Disapproval*, at
his moment of greatest erotic triumph, to soar instead of being confined
to laboured jokes about veal. ... The strength of *Woman in Mind* is its
concentration on Susan. Firmly on her side, it still shows her as a col-
laborator in her own destruction, and a contributor to that of others as
well.

Robert Cushman, *Plays International*, Oct. 1986, p. 23

The central character of Alan Ayckbourn's latest play is one of the most
moving and devastating that he has created. ... As Ayckbourn digs
relentlessly deeper into her psyche the farce becomes more bizarre, so
the volume of laughter increases to block out pain until the last,
lingering moment as she sinks into incoherence. Who else has the nerve,
the assurance, and the accomplishment to leave us on such a downbeat

of despair, by way of such merriment? Who else could turn the dramatic cliché of a knock on the head into such a compassionate study of the damage we unthinkingly, unfeelingly, do to each other?

> Robin Thornber, 'Savage Spirit of the Family',
> *The Guardian*, 1 June 1985

The problem with Ayckbourn is two-fold. His characters are so brilliantly sketched that we end up liking even the most loathsome of them; and he does not manipulate them into the reassurance of a happy ending. Part of the excitement in his writing is the way he confounds all one's expectations. ... His point is that unhappiness and frustrated exuberance can drive people to create a fantasy world for themselves, and that in time that world will make its own terrible demands. This being an English middle-class comedy, fantasy is a matter of class: in a better world people have better accents and more refined vocabulary; they are gently ruthless but imperiously amorous.

> John Peter, 'The Serious Art of British Farce',
> *Sunday Times*, 10 Sept. 1986, p. 47

Ayckbourn is a past master at having one stage space simultaneously represent different places, but now for the first time he has a real and an unreal world interpenetrate ever more amusingly and alarmingly. ... The play goes from the hilariously downbeat to the comically macabre and, without switching gears, to the suddenly moving. It is also a sensitive, accurate, and touching portrayal of someone losing touch with reality, a reality the soberest judge must concede to be pretty untouchable and not a little demented. What is Susan to do, beset by a husband who, as their son puts it, is 'not a man of few words where several spring to mind', a sister-in-law who insists on cooking but can't tell a tea from a *fine herbe* and produces 'burnt Earl Grey omelettes'?. ... And then that other family, so sophisticated, affluent, and doting on Susan — how diametrically opposite their imaginary virtues are to the scurvy substantiality they put to utter shame. It would be madness to choose sanity here. Yet Ayckbourn doesn't cheat: Susan cannot be trusted as an arbiter, and her escape is no less heartbreaking than what she is escaping from . ... *Woman in Mind* teaches us to shed our facile certainties.

> John Simon, 'British Twilight, American Fog',
> *New York*, 29 Feb. 1988, p. 120-1

See also:
Bernard F. Dukore, 'Craft, Character, Comedy: Ayckbourn's *Woman in Mind*', *Twentieth Century Literature*, XXXII (Spring 1986), p. 23-39.

A Small Family Business

A play in two acts.
First London production: Olivier Th., 21 May 1987 (dir. Ayckbourn;
    with Michael Gambon as Jack and Simon Cadell as Hough; later
    Stephen Moore as Jack and Clive Francis as Hough).
Published: Faber, 1987; French, 1987.

The play is a tale of corruption in a family furniture business.
Jack McCracken gives up his job in a frozen-food merchants to
run the firm set up by his ailing father-in-law. As he discovers, it
is a great leap from fish fingers to fitted wardrobes. At the party
given him by his relatives, he delivers an idealistic little speech
about how he intends to instil 'basic trust' in the firm. No petty
thieving for a start, for the larger fraud grows from the smaller
theft of the office paper-clip. The speech earns polite applause
from the assembled company whose own collective activities are
to lead Jack into corpse disposal and international drug-
dealing. The parable of the paper-clip is borne out very quickly.
Jack's innocence is compromised almost as soon as his
adolescent daughter is caught shop-lifting by a truly reptilian
private investigator called Hough. Jack offers Hough a job
investigating his own company and gets his daughter off the
charge. But Hough begins to uncover fraud on a huge scale,
involving just about every member of the family, masterminded
by Jack's kinky sister-in-law Anita, and including five randy
Italian brothers, all of whom are Anita's lovers. ...
    Christopher Edwards, 'Polite Applause', *Spectator*, 13 June 1987, p. 46

Writing with the Olivier in mind, I had my mind set on the scale and the
sort of subject necessary to sustain it, and I came up with the idea of a
'modern morality play'. My son had been studying catering, and he was
telling me about all the tricks of accounting, what you regularly have to
write off every day. And there I was feeling like a complete idiot, asking
all those old fuddy-duddy questions like 'You mean they steal food from
the kitchens? Why don't they stop them? Why don't they pay them
more, and then dismiss them if they are caught doing anything
dishonest?' And so I decided to write this morality about a man who
decides to run his family business on lines of absolute honesty, paying
people what they deserve and then expecting them to take not so much

77

as a paper-clip, being absolutely straight with the tax people and so on. Of course it is a sort of tragedy. First one of his family gets into trouble, and, his duties as a father coming first, he has to bend the rules a little bit. And once he has started, one thing leads inevitably to another, until by the end he is involved in heavy drug-smuggling, the works. And all through this, we have to sympathise with him and condone what he is doing every step of the way. What the play's really about is the virtual non-existence of set moral codes any more, and the fallacy of trying to live by one. I think now the only thing we can do — and in a way cannot help doing — is to make up our own moral codes as we go along, following out our feelings that 'I would do this, but I would draw the line at that'. The conclusion the play leads to, I might say, is the purely practical one of 'You can take the paper-clips, but draw the line at the desk'. I suppose that's why, in the end, it's a comedy, not a tragedy. I suppose that's why all my plays are.

Ayckbourn, quoted by John Russell Taylor, 'Scarborough's Prodigy', *Plays and Players*, April 1987, p. 10

[*A Small Family Business*], while purporting to be an onslaught upon the new materialism and the way in which the enterprise culture panders to greed, is in fact a farce based upon dubious premises. It is powered by a sequence of laboured devices and the kind of stereotyped and caricaturist character painting in which he excels. For Ayckbourn's family suburbia is just as predictable as the famous models of suburbia — like those of Priestley and N.C. Hunter — which have preceded them. His novelties are principally technical. ... I am not persuaded by the likelihood of this portrait of an acquisitive family up to its eyeballs in fraud directed against itself, but it does give Ayckbourn a chance to show his old familiar parade of wives and husbands afflicted by sexual alienation or loss of erotic desire or even concern for each other. ... The crude laboriousness of these vignettes runs in parallel to Jack's instant venality, which culminates in Mafia tactics and murder. Ayckbourn's indictment of the acquisitiveness and the greedy is ruined by the coarse exaggeration of his indictments. ... It is Simon Cadell as the Uriah Heep-like Hough, with his woebegone moustache and quavering voice, a snail-like creep of a hunched walk, head quizzically tilted, and bird-like eyes, who actually makes caricature seem gloriously apt.

Nicholas de Jongh, *The Guardian*, 8 June 1987

The farceur in Ayckbourn may stop it from being as powerful as it should be. ... He seems to be writing (or is it only the ambience of the National Theatre that makes us feel this?) a tract for the times, an indictment of national dishonesty. I wouldn't dispute his diagnosis, but his characterization is a little thin to support it. For the first time he seems to have run out of grisly suburban types, and has to re-cycle them from earlier plays. The voracious Anita, entertaining the five Italian brothers (all played by the same actor) with whom the family does its dirty business, is a black-leather re-run of the man-eating wife in *A Chorus of Disapproval*. ... Jack himself, despite his impressive early confrontation with the detective — impressive both in its strength and in the obstinacy that hints at ultimate weakness — is something of a lay-figure. He has to resist, and then he has to surrender, repeatedly; otherwise there would be no play.

Robert Cushman, *Plays International*, July 1987, p. 26

As characters, Ayckbourn's people are fearful. They have the marks of hatred on them. Obsessive, anorexic, dog-loving Harriet; greedy, food-connoisseuring Desmond; and possession-wise, fat, complaisantly cuckolded Cliff, a business executive with the ethics of a Maltese pimp — they are transcendentally horrible people. Every previous excursion by the author into human fallibility looks like a trip round the bay compared to this voyage of disabuse. ... The play actually suffers from the author's skills. His little boast is that if a cup of tea has to be got from one side of the stage to the other, he can usually manage it. On this occasion he manages Samantha's tragedy of self-destruction, and makes it dreadfully real in circumstances where there is no room for it. To be bearable, these grotesques must be masques and humours. Intolerably and hurtfully, Samantha turns real, with veins to take needles.

Edward Pearce, 'Death on Stage', *Encounter*, Feb. 1988, p. 70

As in all the best farces, greed and embarrassment are the primary fuels on which these people run. But where, say, Feydeau's characters are driven by greed which they struggle feebly to suppress, being cruelly blocked by embarrassment, Ayckbourn's learn triumphantly to ignore the second while surrendering unconditionally to the first. Feydeau's characters are innocents in a world paved with good intentions. There are no good intentions in Ayckbourn. It is innocence itself that is venal, culpable and inevitably bound to cause trouble.

Hilary Spurling, 'Changing Places',
Times Literary Supplement, 19 June 1987, p. 663

Henceforward

A play in two acts.

First production: Stephen Joseph Th., Scarborough, 30 July 1987
  (dir. Ayckbourn; with Barry McCarthy as Jerome).
First London production: Vaudeville Th., 16 Nov. 1988.
First American production: Alley Th., Houston, 4 Oct. 1987
  (dir. Ayckbourn; with George Segal as Jerome and Judy Geeson
  as Zoe).

The play is a cynical space-age comedy about a world that, according to the author's dire prophecy, is not very distant. This will be a time of overly automated man and out-of-control computers, each fighting for dominance. On the most immediate level, the play deals with an artist's block. ... His protagonist is an avant-garde *composer, a synthesizer of overheard human sounds. He is a kind of musical* voyeur, *or 'listening Tom', and his invasion of the privacy of others remains an unsettling motif throughout the evening. He has sequestered himself in a hi-tech bunker in a London suburb. Besieged by a marauding army of Amazons, creatures from a cyber-punk nightmare, he shields himself with a complex security system that includes welded shutters and a video-phone answering machine that always seems to be on fast forward. Attending to his needs is a malfunctioning female android (one of the author's cleverest creations). Further complicating the plot is the composer's plan to regain custody of his daughter, lost to him during his breakup with his wife. The comedy is futuristic-domestic, as the composer tries to use the latest in technology in order to solve his personal and creative crises. His instrument in this quest is an actress, whom he hires to help him project an image of household bliss for a social worker from the Department of Child Well-Being.*

Mel Gussow, 'New from Ayckbourn', *New York Times*, 11 Oct. 1987

Two questions are proposed, half seriously and unanswerably, by this gentle Frankenstein. Are machines better than people? Justin cannot of course say that they are, but given the kind of friends and family he has and the fact that Ayckbourn's characters are so often programmed with the devious banalities of received opinion and daily life, neither can he definitely say they are not. What does love sound like? Justin wants to discover a sound so perfect and precise it will be recognized at once. The answer turns out to be the sound for the word 'love', plain spoken into his face with merciless clarity by Corinna, then distorted ingeniously but decadently by his machines. ... It is a cool, clever, doodling kind of play, intermittently funny, but excessively long and with no kind of solid emotional ground (unlike, say, *Chorus of Disapproval*) between soft sentimentality and hard ice.

Michael Ratcliffe, 'Black Soul in a Suitcase',
The Observer, 9 Aug. 1987, p. 19

This is a fable not of social observation but personal obsession: in particular that of artistic self-hatred. The world it conjures up is that of a man who, for the sake of his work, has neglected human ties and barricaded himself into a creative cell, only to discover that he has cut off his creative sources. The play makes the doubly despairing statement that human beings do each other so much damage that they would be better off living with amiably programmed machines; and that, without human models, even machines expire like the finally exhausted Nan. In telling this essentially one-character story, Ayckbourn resorts to several abrupt changes in narrative direction. He also succeeds yet again in discovering achingly funny means of expressing extreme distress.

Irving Wardle, *The Times*, 1 Aug. 1987, p. 18

The most original and unsettling English comedy since Peter Nichols's *A Day in the Death of Joe Egg*. ... This play is full of disconcerting surprises. It is as if the Mary Shelley of *Frankenstein* had collaborated with the Anthony Burgess of *Clockwork Orange* on a raucous, malevolent comedy of masculine inadequacy and social failure. The mixture may sound strange, but it works with lethal efficiency. After all, most really good science fiction skirts the edge of comedy; and the best (Shelley, Stevenson, Vonnegut, Ballard) are moral parables in which the fantastic becomes horribly real, and nothing is but what is not. Ayckbourn the moralist is scoring some unsettling and sobering points. One is that if men treat women like dummies, they themselves will become so unfeeling that only dummies will seem to them like women. Another is that urban man is driving himself into a corner where efficiency becomes more important than morality or feeling.

John Peter, 'Ayckbourn's Lethal Mixture',
Sunday Times, 2 Aug. 1987, p. 43

Man of the Moment

First production: Stephen Joseph Th., Scarborough, 10 Aug. 1988 (dir. Ayckbourn).

b: Revues

Men on Women on Men

Short late-night revue: music by Paul Todd.
First production: Stephen Joseph Th., Scarborough, 17 June 1978.
Unpublished; cassette (TSJTITR 001) issued by Stephen Joseph Th.

On to this 'fifties form Ayckbourn has honed a 'seventies cutting edge. Items which in themselves seem quite trite have a cumulative effect — 'life's gay love song tends to finish as a dirge' — which is as simply, subtly breathtaking as a thump in the gut. Having rescued farce from being a term of abuse, can he now claim the mantle of Sandy Wilson as well as that of Ben Travers? On the matter of marriage, Ayckbourn is of course at home. In this less familiar form, his blow-by-blow ring-side commentary from the matrimonial arena becomes despatches from the front of the sex war. Each sketch signals its position in the opening lines with a well-worn phrase or saying which transfixes an attitude, an accommodation, a lifestyle, and then defines the lines of battle, recounts the ploys, and lists the casualties. ... David Millard's setting of 14 shop-lifter mirrors and a wire cage brings to the theatre's bursting bar — in a converted classroom — a golden afterglow of decadence.

Robin Thornber, *The Guardian*, 19 June 1978

First Course

Music by Paul Todd
First production: Stephen Joseph Th., Scarborough, 8 July 1980.

Second Helping

Music by Paul Todd.
First production: Stephen Joseph Th., Scarborough, 5 Aug. 1980.

Me, Myself and I

Music by Paul Todd. Three linked lunch-time shows, staged together in London.

First production: Stephen Joseph Th., Scarborough. *Me* opened on
  2 June 1981, *Myself* on 8 July and *I* on 9 July.
First London production: Orange Tree, Richmond, 10 Dec. 1982
  (dir. Kim Grant).

As polished and witty a chamber musical as any I have seen in a long
time. Mrs. Mary Yately is no ordinary housewife. She is the *Evening
Echo*'s Ideal Mum of the Year. More than that, she exists in triplicate.
Much to the confusion of Rodney Beech, who comes to interview her,
she has two *alter egos*, Myself and I, who chatter irrepressibly in the
background, undermining her confidence, egging her on to indiscretions
and commenting caustically on her male interviewers. They resent being
patronized as a housewife, these two inner selves. Regularly they take
her place at the pub table and throw her discretion to the winds,
titillating Rodney with lurid tales of Twickenham wife-swapping and
putting the fear of God into his bragging, male chauvinist boss with a
brazen invitation to sex. By the time her husband arrives to take her
home, they have given Mary enough courage to stick up for herself and
get him back into line. ... Peter Gale plays the men in Mary's life — the
ingenuous cub reporter, his conceited, self-satisfied boss, and her
overbearing husband.

Christopher Hudson, Evening Standard, 11 Dec. 1982

Incidental Music

Music by Paul Todd. Eighty-minute revue.
First production: Stephen Joseph Th., Scarborough, 12 Jan. 1983.
First London production: Orange Tree, Richmond, 2 Dec. 1983
  (dir. Martin Connor).

It's a sort of revue with the sketches built into the musical numbers, a
dozen staged songs, unconnected, but mostly on the familiar Ayckbourn
theme of bittersweet human relationships slickly done on a thrust stage
surrounded with candlelit cabaret tables. There's a simple, moving,
lyrical love song, 'The Voices', and 'Lover Cycle', a sort of sung sketch
version of *La Ronde*; a mini murder mystery and a fresh treatment of the
well worn agony column theme. 'Much Good' is about those people
who are too good for this world, 'living as we do'. Even in this
shorthand format Ayckbourn's humour comes through his characters and
situations rather than the words alone, and so the most successful are the

most substantial, where there's time for these things to develop. 'Round of Drinks' is just that — cocktail party conversation sliced into stanzas with each character's dialogue sung solo before they are all blended. 'Schoolfriends' is one of those disastrous reunions of people who have grown apart. And 'Petra and the Wolves' is a hilarious send-up of the fairytale world. Sophistication is what it's all about — in content and style. ... Todd's music is laid-back Radio Two.

Robin Thornber, *The Guardian*, 14 Jan. 1983

Seven Deadly Virtues

Music by Paul Todd.
First production: Stephen Joseph Th., Scarborough, 12 Jan. 1984
(dir. Ayckbourn).

The shows take the form of a series of sung sketches, each with its own story to tell, related to a common theme. This time it's a hooded look at the so-called natural virtues of fortitude, prudence, justice and temperance, and the supernatural faith, hope and charity. It opens, typically, with a couple of revellers whistling in the dark while demons appear behind them on Edward Lipscomb's set of split-level platforms and stairs. It closes, typically, with the funeral of a business tycoon rejecting the smothering 'charity' of his mother, wife and secretary from an afterlife where he can stop playing roles. ... Todd's music was more moodily varied than ever before.

Robin Thornber, *The Guardian*, 14 Jan. 1984

The Westwoods

Music by Paul Todd.
First production: Stephen Joseph Th., Scarborough, 24, 29 and 31 May 1984.
First London production: Etcetera Th., Oxford Arms, 19 May 1987
(dir. Vivienne Cozens).

Four stages in the life of Patricia Westwood, played by four actresses: pony-tailed Tidge in the 'fifties trying to coax some emotion out of sullen schoolboy Robert; mini-skirted Patricia shacking up with pop merchant Rab; matronly Trish knowing all about husband Bobby's affair with a girl half his age; menopausal Pat astonished by a schoolboy's calf-love for her. When the plot requires the on-stage presence of Tidge's mother, Trish's daughter or father's girlfriend the plot allows an actress of the needed age-group to be on hand to play her. It is no surprise to learn that in the second act Ayckbourn shows us the male side of the coins, four actors playing a succession of Roberts. New encounters echo the old, with a different player commenting on events. So a schoolboy thrilled that an older woman appreciates his Doris Day records is matched thirty years later when he thrills her by bringing her coke to sniff as a birthday treat.

Jeremy Kingston, *The Times*, 30 May 1987, p. 18

Boy Meets Girl, Girl Meets Boy

Music by Paul Todd. Linked lunch-time shows.
First production: Stephen Joseph Th., Scarborough, 23 and 25 May 1985.

Mere Soup Songs

Music by Paul Todd.
First production: Stephen Joseph Th., Scarborough, 22 May 1986.
First London production: Lyttleton Th. buffet, 13 Dec. 1986.

A late-night cabaret on the theme of not telling the truth. Expect nothing harsh. Ayckbourn's songs and dialogue play gently with accusations and denials of infidelity in the gardens and bedrooms of commuter land. Perhaps theatregoers emerging from *King Lear* will be glad to relax over a glass of port, idly wondering if Michael really is having an affair with Charles's wife. Michael denies it, Janice denies it; Charles later denies that he accused him. ... There are more felicities of middle-class chat and put-down but as a comment on the ambiguities of life the incidents forfeit all credence once we have detected the first crucial lie.

Irving Wardle, *The Times*, 15 Dec. 1986, p. 11

c: Television Plays

Service Not Included

Thirty minutes.
First transmitted: 'Masquerade', BBC-2, 20 May 1974
   (dir. Herbert Wise).
Unpublished.

The fancy dress party to which Mr. Ayckbourn invited us marked the
end of the UBS conference, one of those business men's blether
sessions, all bonhomie and back stabbing, which are guaranteed to bore
the pants off anyone who isn't a dedicated company man. The initials
UBS were not explained but the hall porter (Alan Wilson) at Magpie
Manor Hotel, which housed these goings-on, did suggest that they meant
Useless Bunch of So-and-sos, a fairly apt definition as it turned out.
Colin Farrell, playing Donald, the most truly dedicated company man
present, got right into the flesh and bone of the character. Dressed in the
costume of an alpine peasant, which later, in servile agreement with his
boss, he conceded might be Dutch, he spent his evening planning how to
get a word with Warwick, the boss (Clive Morton), and how to present
his carefully-prepared suggestion for replanning the company's
advertising. Freda (Ann Beach), growing maudlin and later sick in the
hotel bath, pleaded in vain with the creepy Donald to put in a word with
Warwick for her husband Neil (Julian Curry), a man who seemed to the
sadly misled Freda to be unaccountably overlooked by his buddies. Neil,
on the pretext of going off to dance, had stolen quietly upstairs with
Cathy (Irene Hamilton), and fortified with champagne, was proceeding
to make a cuckold of clever Donald and a fool of faithful Freda. Around
this central situation the other guests talked, danced and drank with that
unbuttoned abandon of business men on a binge. The hotel staff served
them and observed them with that cynical knowingness peculiar to the
catering trade the world over.

James Scott, 'Enjoyable Half-hour', *The Stage*, 23 May 1974, p. 19

Half an hour, actually, is twenty-eight pages: it's really a night's work.
So I said: 'Well, look, I must see the producers. I must talk about this,
because I don't know anything about it'. So they dutifully showed me
round the studios. And I said: 'Well, could you just give me some idea
of the cast requirements and the set?' And they said: 'We've got this
wonderful new lightweight video camera, so really, don't worry about

the sets. You write what you want to do in half an hour: we will film it.'
I said: 'Oh, that's wonderful. What about cast?' They said: 'You write
what you want: we will cast it. We don't want you to be hampered by
physical conditions. Just write.' So I went away and I wrote this play for
twenty-four people. It roved all over this bloody hotel: there were about
thirty-eight sets. So, silence. 'Ah,' they said, 'Well, we didn't think
you'd write twenty-four people.' So I cut it down to eighteen and
simplified the sets. But, of course, the budget of the series was already
costed and so the whole thing was pitifully under-financed. And,
because of the technical complexities which I'd set, Herbie [Wise], on
location — two days in a pub in Berkshire — was having his work cut
out: some scenes he never got in the can at all, because he had no time!
So, it was OK, but it was very far from what it was originally intended
to be — a waiter's eye-view of a dreadful office party. I didn't find it
very enjoyable.

Ayckbourn, *Conversations*, p. 105

A Cut in the Rates

Twenty-minute comedy.
First transmitted: BBC TV Schools, 21 Jan. 1984.
Unpublished.

A woman housing officer has a nightmare experience with a mad
illusionist who saws women in half.

3. Non-Dramatic Writing

Occasional Poets, ed. Richard Adams (Viking, 1986) [includes poems
by Ayckbourn].

This is a small selection from a large body of material. Ayckbourn has cleverly and uniquely produced the first commentary on his work ahead of critical books, in the form most appropriate to a playwright, dialogue, in Conversations with Ayckbourn, *by Ian Watson (1981). He has written short but informative prefaces to the four collections of his work, though he comments that he will not do this again. As well as a lecture given in 1987, he has given an unusually large number of interviews, as recorded in the Bibliography.*

I'd like to finish up writing tremendously human comedies — Chekhovian comedy in a modern way. ... Light comedy must be recognizable to people in the street. The difficulty is to make it relevant and still funny.

> Interviewed by Robin Thornber,
> 'Farceur, Relatively Speaking',
> *The Guardian*, 7 Aug. 1970

They're all about fairly well-to-do people. My step-father was a bank manager and the milieu that I remember from childhood stays with me. What's more important, though, is that they are all about characters I like. I take them quite seriously. And if you do that you can dig up all sorts of things about them. You can even allow them some unhappiness.

> Interviewed by Philip Oakes, 'Lines and Deadlines',
> *Sunday Times*, 3 June 1973

Significant Theatre, Serious Theatre, are deadly words. They should all be banished, this feeling that unless there is a glum silence in the auditorium, nothing meaningful can be happening. ...

I made a vow when I was an actor with nothing to do except wait for my line on p. 49, that in my plays there would be no butlers, waiters or soldiers with spears.

> Interviewed by Mel Gussow, 'Ayckbourn, Ex-Actor,
> Now Plays Singular Writer of Comedies',
> *New York Times*, 11 Oct. 1974, p. 30

The characters aren't necessarily getting nastier, but I do feel that they're getting sadder. ... I've always thought of comedies as tragedies that have been interrupted. ... I want to write a comedy about loneliness which, in itself, is not funny. But the way I write tends to make such subjects funny, or at least makes them appear so. That is because one sees things from a certain angle. I think I'd be wrong to sit down and conscientiously try *not* to be funny.

Interviewed by Michael Coveney, 'Scarborough Fare',
Plays and Players, Sept. 1975, p. 18-19

I've got an awful lot of Congreve and Oscar Wilde. I've also got a good collection of Chekhov. I think one starts by copying other people. ... Pinter came and worked with us in our company and directed his *Birthday Party* with us. That had a very strong effect. I think if you're ever going to develop you take these influences and they disappear into your bloodstream. ... If I did look like a poor man's Harold Pinter it would be dreadful. What I liked when I first came into contact with his work as an actor was, I suspect, that the way you understand him is as a poet. ... He has a love of distorting the everyday phrase, slightly bending it. He bends it more than I do, but I also bend phrases or put them in incongruous positions in speeches, which I hope makes them funny, simply because they seem slightly out of context. ...

One of my problems, I always say, is that my plays are best appreciated if you've had at least one unhappy marriage or at least one unhappy relationship, otherwise you won't know what we're going on about.

Interviewed by Brian Connell,
'Playing for Laughs to a Lady Typist',
The Times, 5 Jan. 1976, p. 5

You can at most make people see their fellows in a new light, and you can make them feel for the characters, without loving them. ... I want to move further into the Chekhovian field, exploring attitudes to death, loneliness, etc. — themes not generally dealt with in comedy.

Interviewed by Oleg Kerensky,
The New British Drama (1977), p. 129

Eighty per cent of the productions I've seen of my plays have always been far too boisterous: that's the British idea of having a good time. ... I'd love to write a truly hilarious dark play.

Interviewed by Ian Watson, 'Ayckbourn of Scarborough',
Municipal Entertainment, 5, May 1978, p. 11

It seems to me a good thing if you can outline some of the small areas of grey angst in people's minds. ... There's a huge change of role [for women] going on at the moment, and for that reason it's a fascinating period to chronicle, but I don't think it's helped every woman. It has helped a few; it has made others schizophrenic and guilty. Because what do they do now? And it's affected men, too — they don't know what they're supposed to be doing, either. ... My characters are assured a certain standard of living — their problems are *actually* living.

Interviewed by Janet Watts,
'Absurd Persons, Plural and Suburban',
The Observer, 4 Mar. 1979, p. 39

[My ambition is] to write a very serious play that makes people laugh all the time, a play in which all the laughter comes from words like yes or no, or even from the pauses between them.

Interviewed by Benedict Nightingale, 'Ayckbourn —
Comic Laureate of Britain's Middle Class',
New York Times, 25 Mar. 1979, Sec. II, p. 1

I'm really showing how sad it is that people can try to be nice and that it sometimes doesn't work. I'm saying that a lot of the worst things that happen in life are the result of well-meaning actions.

Interviewed by William Foster, 'Playwright in the Round',
In Britain, 35, May 1980, p. 24

I'm on a crusade to try and persuade people that theatre can be fun; but every time I start doing that, some hairy bugger from the left comes in and tells them it's instructive, and drives them all out again. If I want to be instructed, I go to night school. I may be instructed in the theatre, but I don't go in there predominantly for instruction: I go in there for entertainment, and of course all the best plays instruct me, or enlighten me — it's a better word than instruct. ... I'm very lucky that my particular level of writing, class-wise, is slap-bang in the middle of the English theatregoing public.

Interviewed by Ian Watson, *Conversations* (1981), p. 108-9

It seems to me that the deeper you go into a character, the sadder the play must inevitably become.

Interviewed by Ray Connolly, 'Ayckbourn, with Music',
Sunday Times, 8 Feb. 1981, p. 32

If you boil down your themes they sound terribly banal. Mainly I want to say things about the fear and distrust people have for each other, the fact that men and women still don't seem to understand each other very well. There are too many people in the world who are likely to leave important decisions they should make until far too late.

> Interviewed by Bryan Appleyard, 'Still Hoping for Heroes',
> *The Times*, 18 Aug. 1982, p. 7

If you write an honest picture about a person, sooner or later you're going to hit bedrock of frustration or disappointment or something. There's a tendency to dodge that when you begin. Farce is a tragedy that's been interrupted. All you do is edit it at the right point. If you let a character's life run on before editing — let's say until he's married ten years — then as a result you'll have a slightly darker, but I hope truer, picture. I've never had any trouble being funny. I spend most of the time now taking out the jokes not putting them in.

> Interviewed by Michael Hickling, 'Absolutely Farcical',
> *Yorkshire Post*, 5 May 1984

Political theatre is usually so busy being political that it forgets to be theatre. People tend to be sublimated to ideas, so you get this consciously two-dimensional cardboard figure coming on and saying, 'I represent capitalism'. And then you get some appalling little chap on the other side of the stage who represents the downtrodden ... oh, God! you think ... and then on comes the singing shop steward to ecstatic applause — and he hasn't got a name! They can't even be bothered to give him a name. Think of all the writers who have given their characters the possibility of a good *and* a bad side. The best political plays hit you without your knowing it. It's so insulting to be shouted at.

> Interviewed by Michael Church, 'Shakespeare of the South Bank',
> *Sunday Times*, 1 June 1986, p. 42

I consider myself a professional director who writes occasionally. After all, I direct for eleven months of the year, and write for only one. ... For the director who also writes it can hardly help being another research project as well, finding out more about people which somehow, some time he is going to use.

> Interviewed by John Russell Taylor, 'Scarborough's Prodigy',
> *Plays and Players*, Apr. 1987, p. 8

There are still things to say about the fear and dislike people have for each other and the fact that members of each sex are like Martians to the other.

> Interviewed by Mark Lawson, 'A Nation of Shoplifters',
> *The Independent*, 20 May 1987, p. 13

At the moment, touch wood, ideas just pop out; as soon as I get one out, another one arrives, so that is nice, but there is always the fear that it won't happen, that there will be The Blank Sheet of Paper. ... The best part of my work is not the clapping, it's the feeling at the end of the evening, that you have given the most wonderful party and those five hundred strangers who came in are feeling better ... I don't know, but they are sort of unified into a whole and that is marvellous.

> Interviewed by Danny Danziger, *All in a Day's Work* (1987)

The trouble with playwriting is that it is beset with rules. I always compare it with furniture making rather than with any other kind of writing. To create a play you need a great knowledge of construction. The whole thing is to hold an audience's attention for two hours. Narrative, character, development and dialogue are all a crucial part of the process. They are basic rules, but only after you have learned them can you consider breaking them. ... I now realize that I have a double obligation: to an audience — one has to entertain them as a practical writer; but one has also to give them something else besides. And balancing these two aspects is a fine, indeed a keen edged manoeuvre. In the end, it is the tight rope that a commercial play has to be willing to tread.

> 'Alan Ayckbourn', *Drama*, No. 1, 1988, p. 6-7

a: Primary Sources

*The plays are only published separately, as recorded in
Section 1, except for ten in which have been collected into
three volumes:*

Joking Apart and Other Plays (1982) [contains also *Just
    Between Ourselves, Ten Times Table* and *Sisterly Feelings*].
The Norman Conquests (Chatto and Windus, 1975; Penguin,
    1977).
Three Plays (Chatto and Windus, 1977; Penguin, 1979)
    [contains *Bedroom Farce, Absurd Person Singular, Absent
    Friends*].

Articles

'Provincial Playwriting', *The Author*, 81 (Spring 1970),
    p. 25-8.
'Alan Ayckbourn', *Drama*, No. 1, 1988, p. 5-7 [lecture].

Interviews

Robin Thornber, 'A Farceur, Relatively Speaking',
    The Guardian, 7 Aug. 1970.
Joan Buck, 'Alan Ayckbourn', *Plays and Players*, Sept. 1972,
    p. 28-9.
Philip Oakes, 'Lines and Deadlines', *Sunday Times*,
    3 June 1973.
Ronald Hayman, 'Alan Ayckbourn', *The Times*, 4 July 1973,
    p. 13.
Ian Jack, 'Unlocal Lad Makes Good', *Sunday Times*,
    30 June 1974, p. 5.
Robin Stringer, 'Scarborough Fare', *Sunday Telegraph*,
    Magazine, 5 Apr. 1974, p. 27-32.
Mel Gussow, 'Ayckbourn, Ex-Actor, Now Plays Singular
    Writer of Comedies', *New York Times*, 11 Oct. 1974, p. 30.
'Q: Mr. A., Is Sex Funny? A: It Depends, with Me It's
    Hilarious', *New York Times*, 20 Oct. 1974, Sec. II, p. 7.
Shiva Naipaul, 'Scarborough — Where to Succeed in Show
    Business', *Radio Times*, 22 Aug. 1975.
Michael Coveney, 'Scarborough Fare', *Plays and Players*,
    Sept. 1975, p. 15-9.
Brian Connell, 'Playing for Laughs to a Lady Typist',
    The Times, 5 Jan. 1976, p. 5.

John Heilpern, 'Striking Sparks off Suburbia', *The Observer*,
    13 Feb. 1977.
Russell Miller, 'The Hit-Man from Scarborough', *Sunday Times*,
    Magazine, 20 Feb. 1977, p. 22-4, 26.
Ian Watson, 'Ayckbourn of Scarborough', *Municipal Entertainment*, 5,
    May 1978, p. 7-17.
Rosemary Say, 'A Playwright on the Prom', *Sunday Telegraph*,
    28 Jan. 1979, p. 9.
Janet Watts, 'Absurd Persons, Plural and Suburban', *The Observer*,
    4 Mar. 1979, p. 39.
Benedict Nightingale, 'Ayckbourn — Comic Laureate of Britain's
    Middle Class', *New York Times*, 25 Mar. 1979, Sec. II, p. 1, 4.
Paul Vallely, 'Radio Fun', *Radio Times,* 11 Aug. 1979, p. 17-8.
Sheridan Morley, 'British Farce, from Travers to Ayckbourn',
    The Times, 20 Nov. 1979, 17 [dialogue between Ayckbourn and
    Ben Travers].
William Foster, 'Playwright in the Round', *In Britain*, 35, May 1980,
    p. 22-4.
Anthony Masters, 'The Essentially Ambiguous Response', *The Times*,
    4 Feb. 1981, p. 8.
Ray Connolly, 'Ayckbourn, with Music', *Sunday Times*, 8 Feb. 1981,
    p. 32.
Ian Watson, *Conversations with Ayckbourn* (Macdonald, 1981).
Robin Thornber, 'Star of the Seaside Show', *The Guardian*,
    23 July 1981, p. 12.
Bryan Appleyard, 'Still Hoping for Heroes', *The Times*, 18 Aug. 1982,
    p. 7
Paul Allen, 'Interview with Alan Ayckbourn', *Marxism Today*,
    Mar. 1983, p. 39-41.
Robert Beaumont, 'A Change of Scene for Ayckbourn', *Yorkshire
    Evening Press*, 24 Oct. 1985.
Michael Hickling, 'Absolutely Farcical', *Yorkshire Post*, 5 May 1984.
Jill Parkin, 'Change of Direction', *Yorkshire Post*, 31 May 1986.
Michael Church, 'Shakespeare of the South Bank', *Sunday Times*,
    1 June 1986, p. 41-2.
Robin Stringer, 'Ayckbourn: Man with a Woman in Mind', *Daily
    Telegraph*, 30 Aug. 1986.
'The Two Alans', *City Limits*, 11-18 Sept. 1986.
Michael Leech, 'National Ayckbourn', *Drama*, No. 4, 1986, p. 9-10.
Andrew Hislop, 'The People to Watch', *The Times*, 5 Nov. 1986, p. 13.
Peter Roberts, 'Ayckbourn on the South Bank', *Plays International*,
    Feb. 1987, p. 18-20, 36-7.
John Russell Taylor, 'Scarborough's Prodigy', *Plays and Players*,
    Apr. 1987, p. 8-10.

Mark Lawson, 'A Nation of Shoplifters', *The Independent*,
20 May 1987, p. 13.

Interview in *All in a Day's Work*, ed. Danny Danziger (London: Fontana,
1987; also in *The Times*, 27 June 1987, p. 13.

Benedict Nightingale, 'A Woman of Two Minds, Both in Turmoil',
New York Times, 14 Feb. 1988, Sec. H, p. 5, 30.

b: Secondary Sources

Books

Michael Billington, *Alan Ayckbourn* (Macmillan, 1983).

Sidney Howard White, *Alan Ayckbourn* (Boston, Mass.: G.K. Hall,
1984; Twayne English Authors).

Articles and Chapters in Books

Guido Almansi, 'Victims of Circumstance: Alan Ayckbourn's Plays',
Encounter, April 1978, p. 58-65; reprinted in *Modern British
Dramatists: New Perspectives*, ed. John Russell Brown (Englewood
Cliffs, N.J.: Prentice-Hall, 1984), p. 109-20.

Elmer M. Blistein, 'Alan Ayckbourn: Few Jokes, Much Comedy',
Modern Drama, XXVI (March 1983), p. 26-35.

Richard Allen Cave, *New British Drama in Performance on the London
Stage, 1970 to 1985* (Gerrards Cross: Colin Smythe, 1987), p. 65-71.

John Elsom, *Post-War British Theatre* (Routledge and Kegan Paul,
1976), p. 193.

Ronald Hayman, *British Theatre since 1955* (Oxford University Press,
1979), p. 68-9.

Harold Hobson, 'Alan Ayckbourn — Playwright of Ineradicable
Sadness', *Drama*, Winter 1982, p. 4-6.

Albert E. Kalsom, 'Alan Ayckbourn', *British Dramatists since World
War II*, Dictionary of Literary Biography, Vol. 13, p. 15-31.

Oleg Kerensky, *The New British Drama* (Hamish Hamilton, 1977),
p. 115-31 [includes short interview].

Malcolm Page, 'The Serious Side of Alan Ayckbourn', *Modern Drama*,
XXVI (March 1983), p. 36-46.

John Russell Taylor, 'Art and Commerce', *Contemporary English
Drama*, ed. C.W.E. Bigsby (Edward Arnold, 1981), p. 176-88 [on
Ayckbourn, Robert Bolt, Simon Gray and Peter Shaffer].

——, 'Only when They Laugh?', *Plays and Players*, Mar. 1982,
p. 15-6 [on Ayckbourn and Michael Frayn].

——, *The Second Wave* (Methuen, 1971), p. 155-62.